PIANO • VOCAL

BROADWAY MUSICALS
Show by Show
2006–2013

ISBN 978-1-4803-6239-0

HAL•LEONARD®
CORPORATION
7777 W. BLUEMOUND RD. P.O. BOX 13819 MILWAUKEE, WI 53213

Visit Hal Leonard Online at
www.halleonard.com

BROADWAY MUSICALS
Show by Show
2006–2013

CONTENTS
Alphabetical by Song

BROADWAY MUSICALS
Show by Show
2006-2013

CONTENTS
Chronological by Show

SHOW OFF
from THE DROWSY CHAPERONE

Words and Music by LISA LAMBERT
and GREG MORRISON

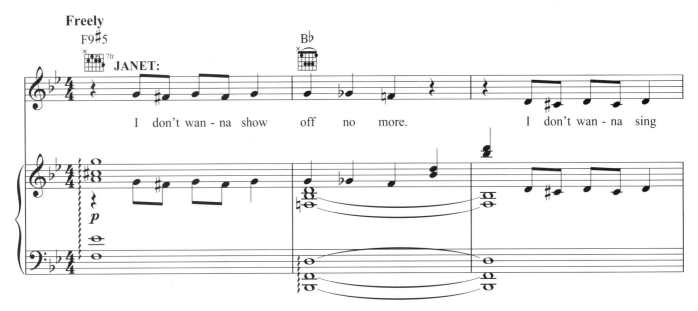

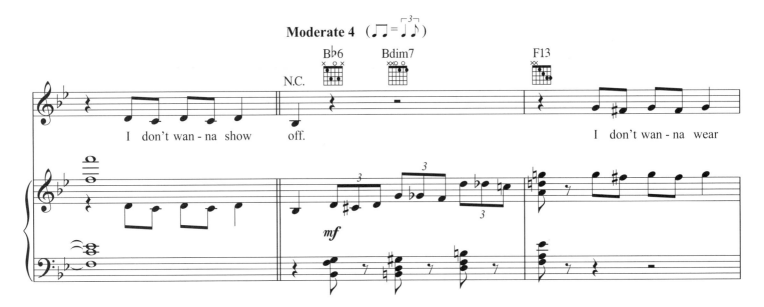

this no more,＿ play the sau - cy Swiss Miss no more,＿

blow my sig - na - ture (kiss) no more. I don't wan - na show

off. Don't try to con - trol me.

I've made up my mind, and that's

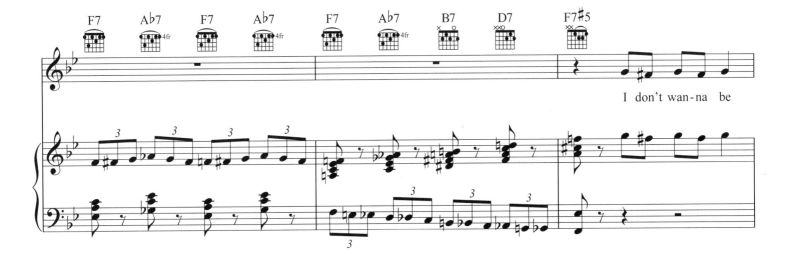

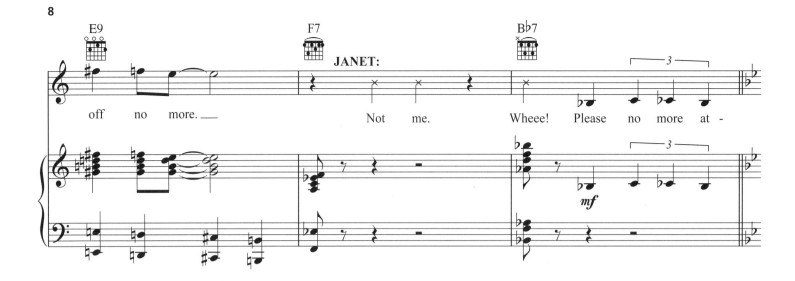

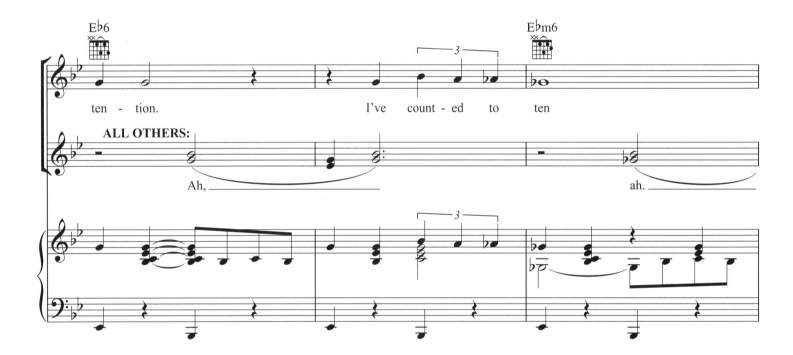

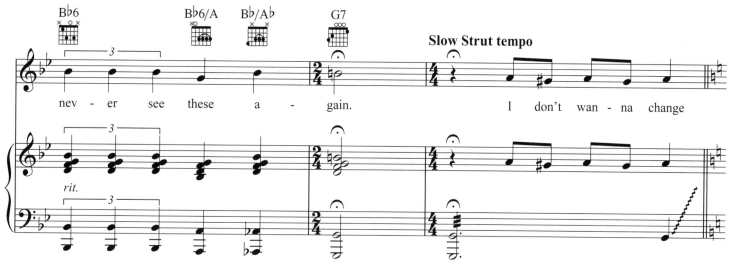

keys no more. _ I don't wan-na strip-tease no more.

accel.

Moderate 4

I don't wan-na say "cheese" no more. I don't care if you

scoff. I don't wan-na be cheered no more, _

praised no more, _ grabbed no more, _ touched no more, _

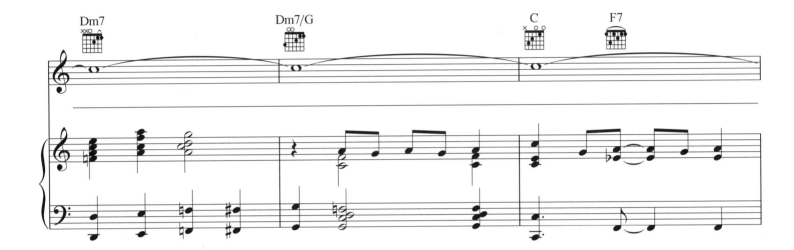

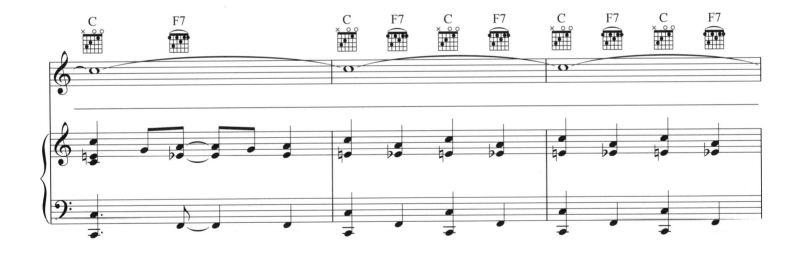

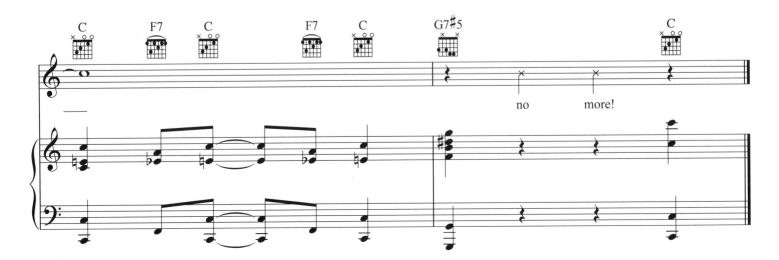

YOU'LL BE IN MY HEART

Disney Presents TARZAN The Broadway Musical

Words and Music by
PHIL COLLINS

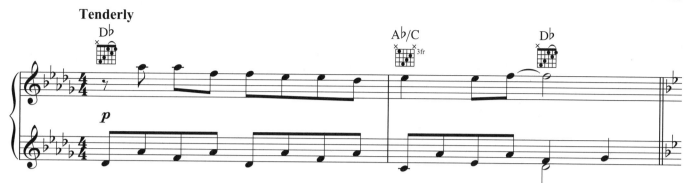

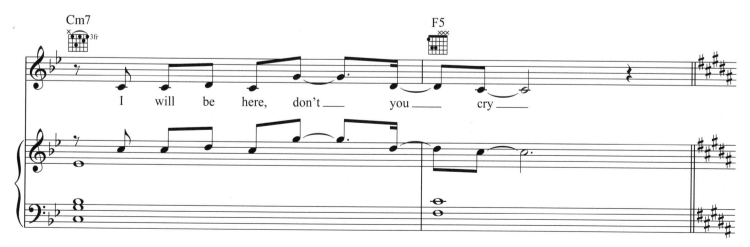

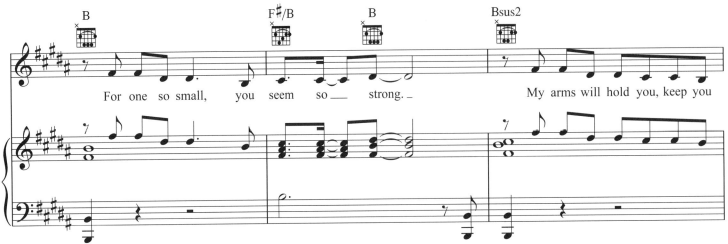

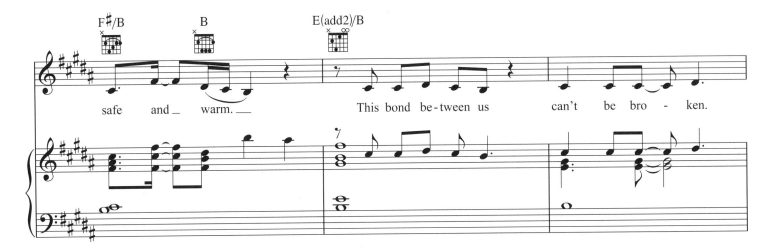

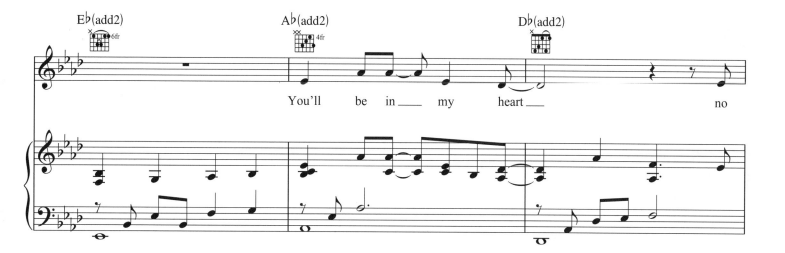

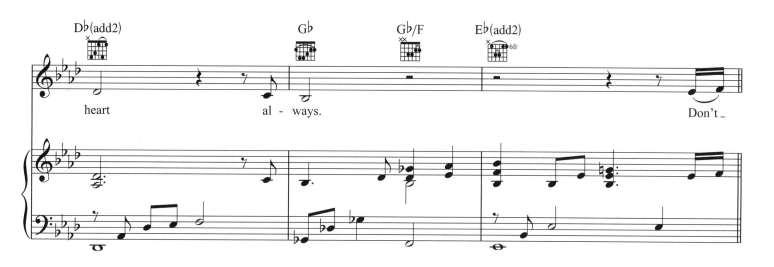

ANOTHER WINTER
IN A SUMMER TOWN
from GREY GARDENS

Music by SCOTT FRANKEL
Lyrics by MICHAEL KORIE

*Original key B major

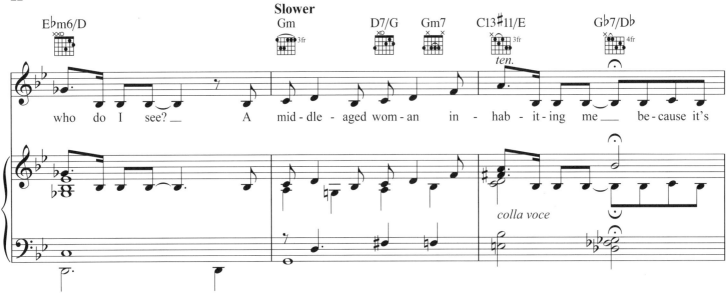

Slower

who do I see?— A mid - dle - aged wom-an in - hab - it-ing me ___ be-cause it's

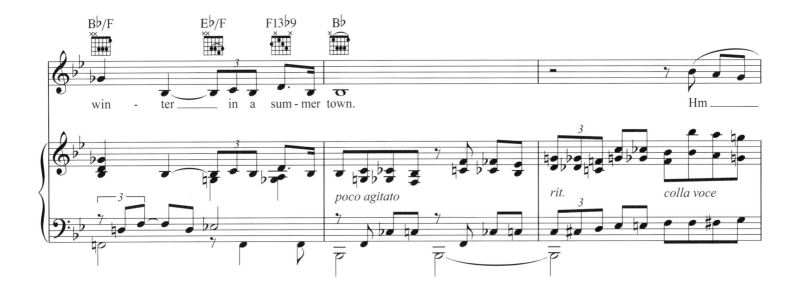

win - ter ___ in a sum - mer town. Hm ___

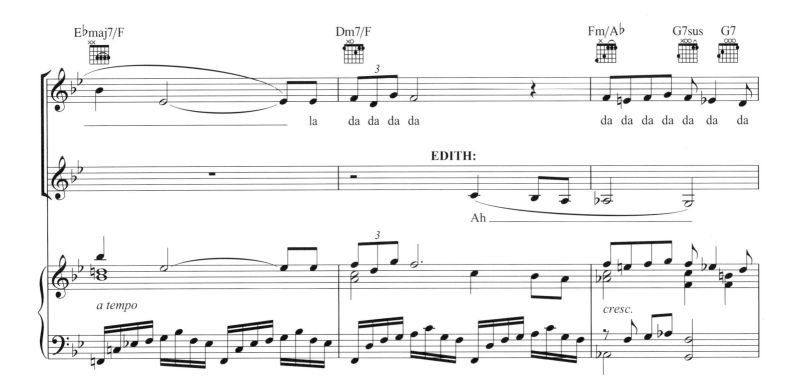

la da da da da da da da da da da da

EDITH:

Ah ___

young Na - vy he - ro; his ten - der em - brace... that sap-phire blue o - cean... oh,

how can I face _ an - oth - er win - ter _____ in a sum - mer town? Oh

God, oh God, my God...

PRACTICALLY PERFECT

from MARY POPPINS

Music by GEORGE STILES
Lyrics by ANTHONY DREWE

sound.   I'm prac - ti - cal - ly per - fect _____ from head to

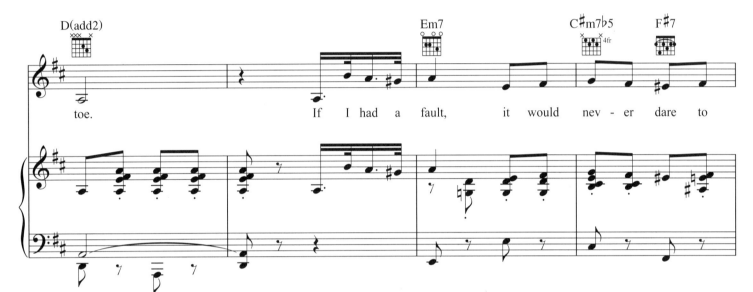

toe.   If I had a fault, it would nev - er dare to

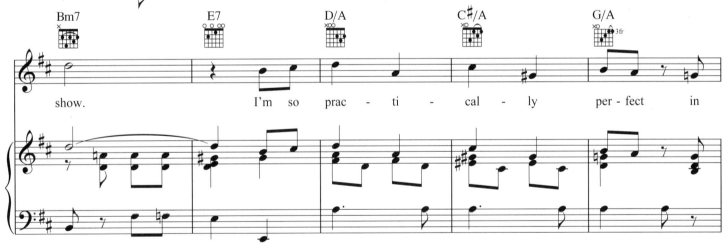

show.   I'm so prac - ti - cal - ly per - fect in

A little faster

ev - e - ry   way. _____

Both prim and pro-per and nev-er too stern. _

_ Well ed-u-cat-ed, yet will-ing to learn. _

_ I'm clean and hon-est, my man-ner re-fined, _

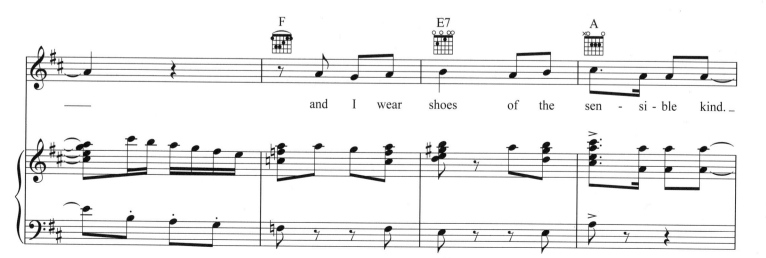

_ and I wear shoes of the sen-si-ble kind. _

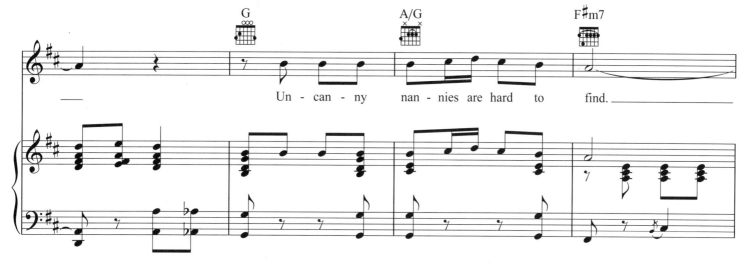

Un - can - ny nan - nies are hard to find.

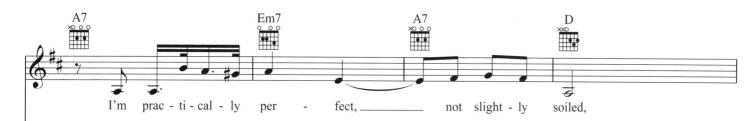

U - nique, yet meek, un - speak - a - bly kind.

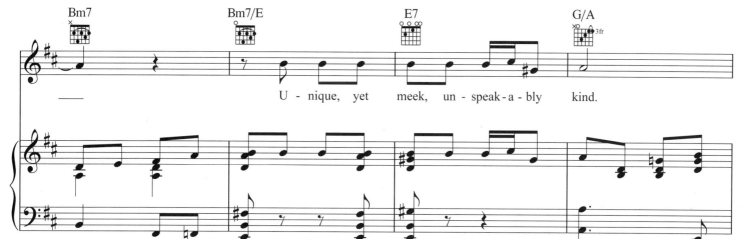

I'm prac - ti - cal - ly per - fect, _____ not slight - ly soiled,

run - ning like an en - gine that's just been fresh - ly oiled.

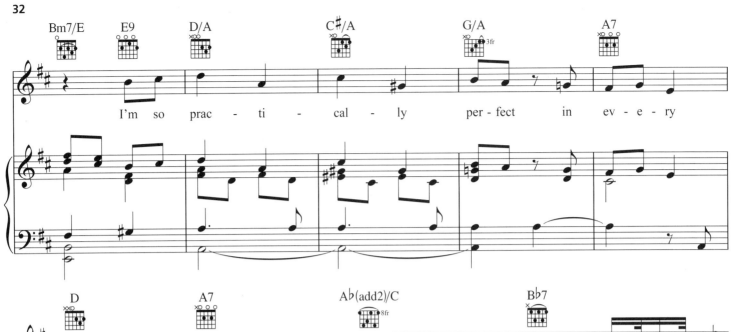

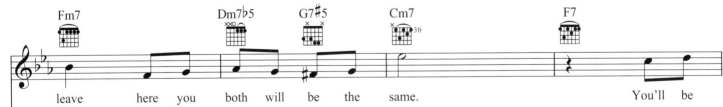

prac - ti - cal - ly per - fect, prac - ti -

cal - ly per - fect. You will be prac - ti - cal - ly

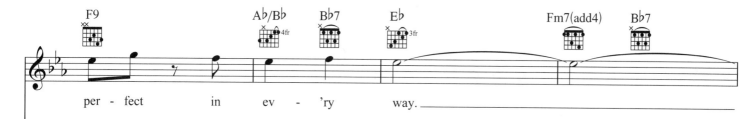

per - fect in ev - 'ry way.

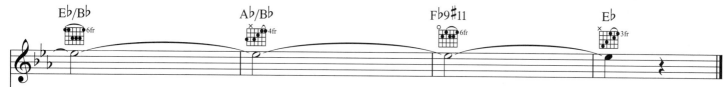

MAMA WHO BORE ME
from SPRING AWAKENING

Music by DUNCAN SHEIK
Lyrics by STEVEN SATER

WENDLA: Ma - ma, _____ who bore _ me, Ma - ma, _____ who gave _ me no way _ to han - dle things, _ who _ made me _ so _____ sad. Ma - ma, _____ the weep - ing, Ma - ma, _____ the an - gels.

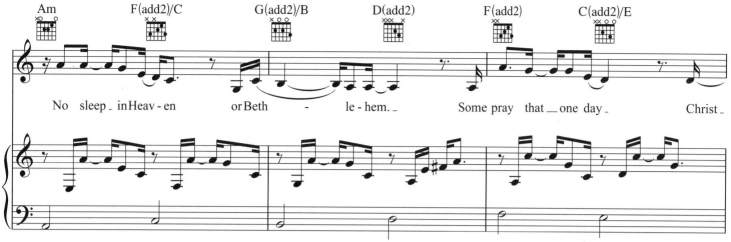

No sleep _ in Heav - en   or Beth -   le - hem. _   Some pray that _ one day _   Christ _

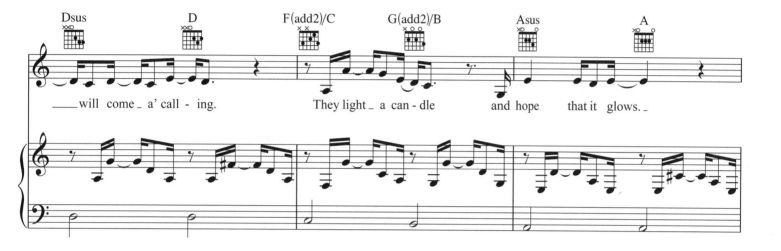

_ will come _ a' call - ing.   They light _ a can - dle   and hope   that it glows. _

And some _ just lie _ there, cry - ing for Him to come _ and find _ them.   But

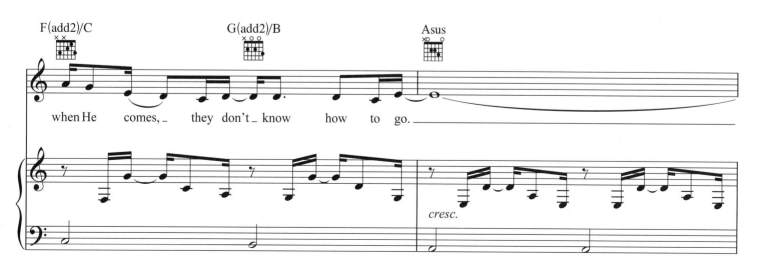

when He   comes, _   they don't _ know   how   to go. _____

cresc.

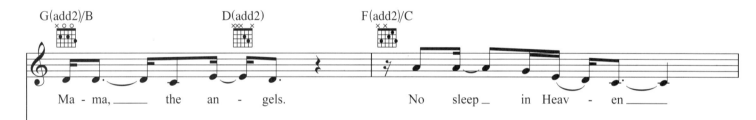

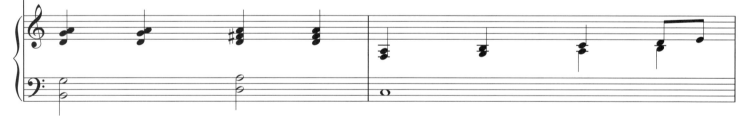

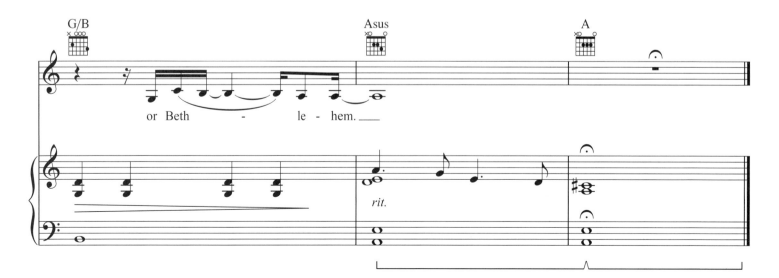

I MISS THE MUSIC

from CURTAINS

Music and Lyrics by
JOHN KANDER

Freely

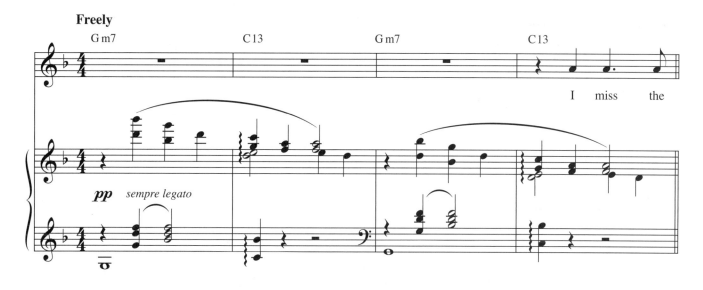

Rubato

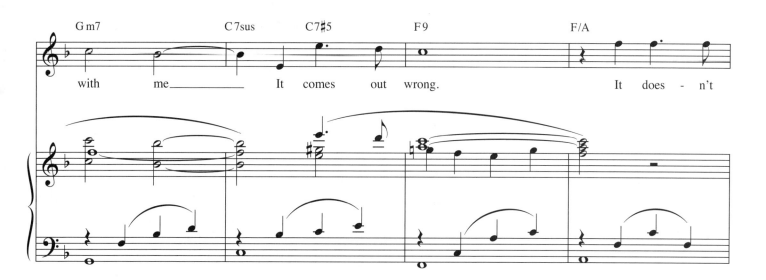

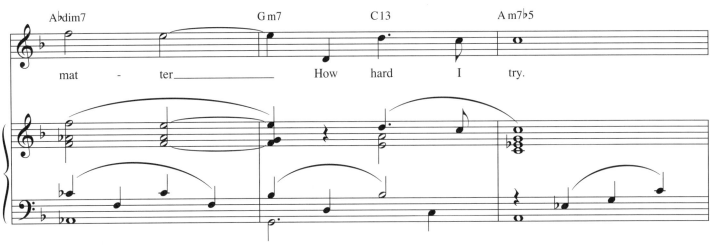

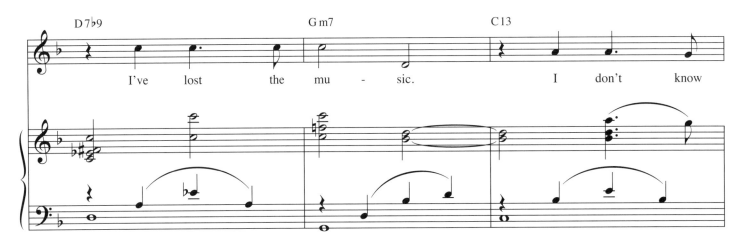

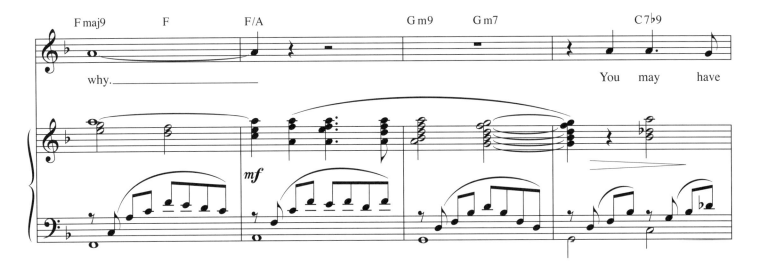

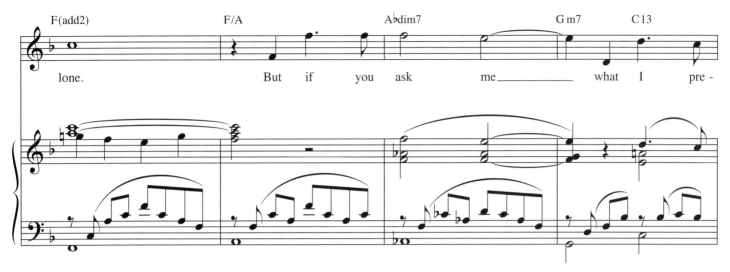

lone. But if you ask me_____ what I pre-

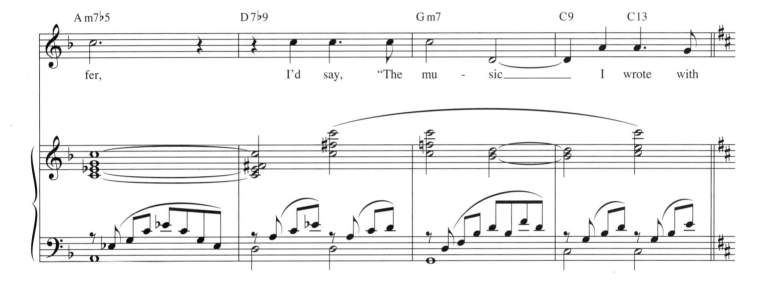

fer, I'd say, "The mu - sic_____ I wrote with

her."   When you're

No one tells you, "That's not fun-ny." No one says, "Let's cut that bar."

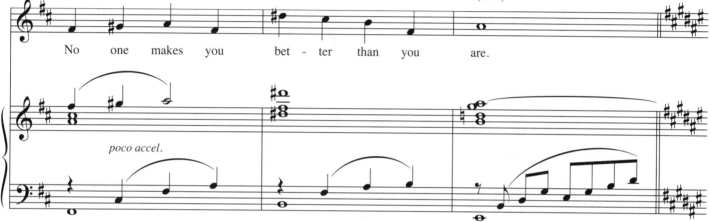

No one makes you bet - ter than you are.

Con poco moto

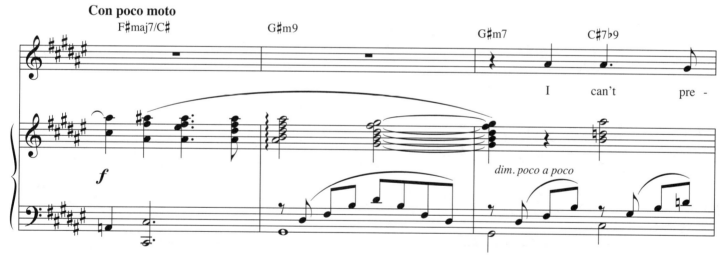

I can't pre -

tend.____ I miss the mu - sic.____ I miss my

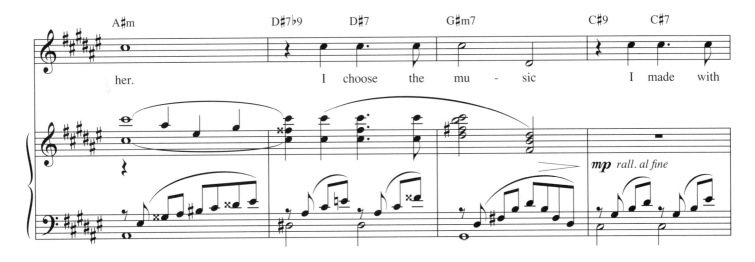

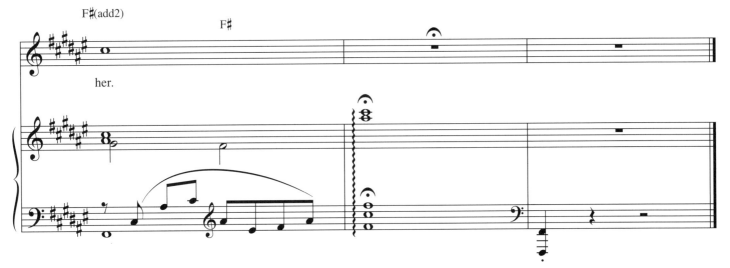

SO MUCH BETTER

from LEGALLY BLONDE

Music and Lyrics by LAURENCE O'KEEFE
and NELL BENJAMIN

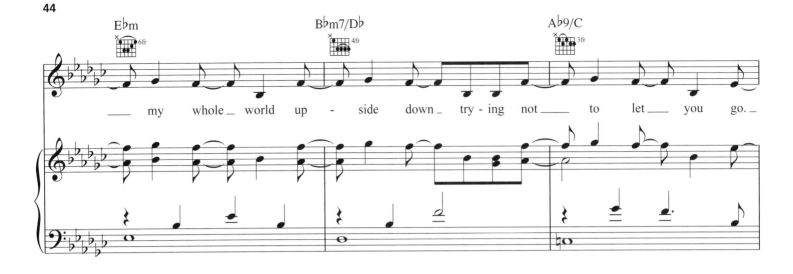

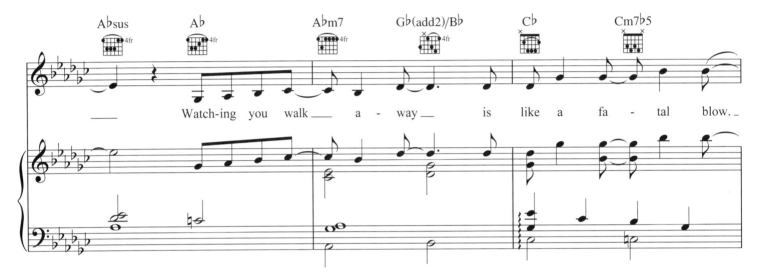

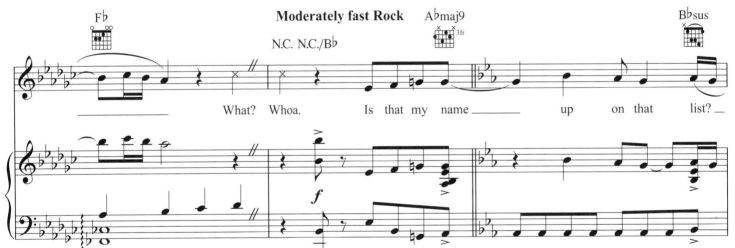

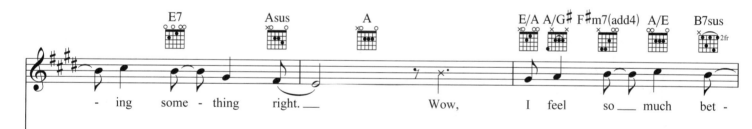

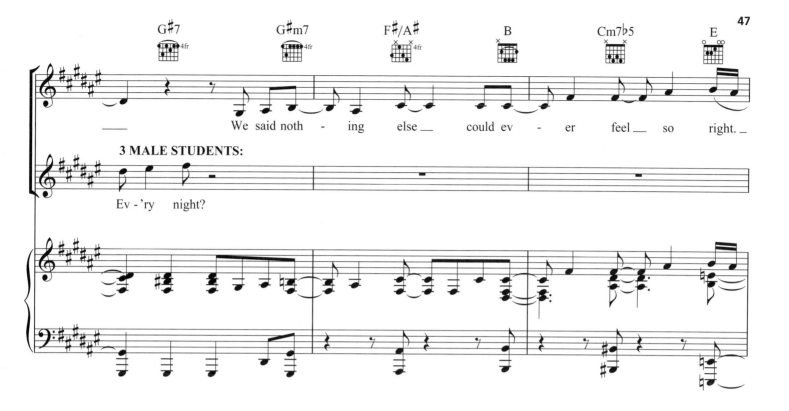

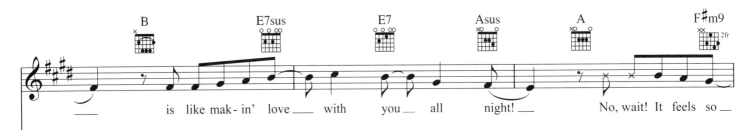

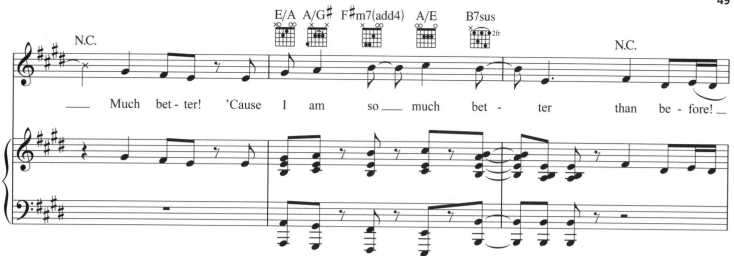

Much bet-ter! 'Cause I am so ___ much bet - ter than be - fore! ___

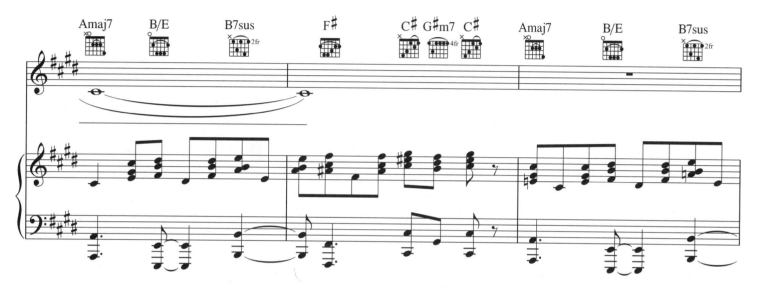

May - be she's what you pre - fer, ___

but hey, last year I was her. ___ May - be you will change your mind, __

ELLE: add CHORUS:

Much bet - ter!" And soon ____ all y'all ____ gon - na know ____

ELLE:

____ much bet - ter that I am so ____ much bet - ter.

CHORUS:

____ much bet - ter! I am so ____ much bet -

I am so ____ much bet - ter, ____ I am so ____ much bet -

- ter, ____ I am so ____ much! I am so ____ much bet -

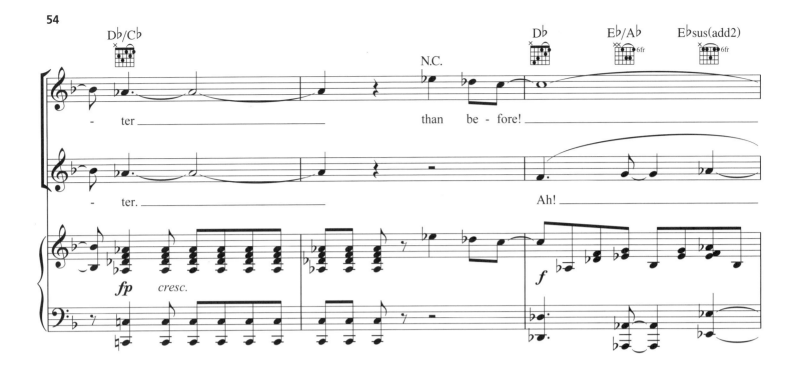

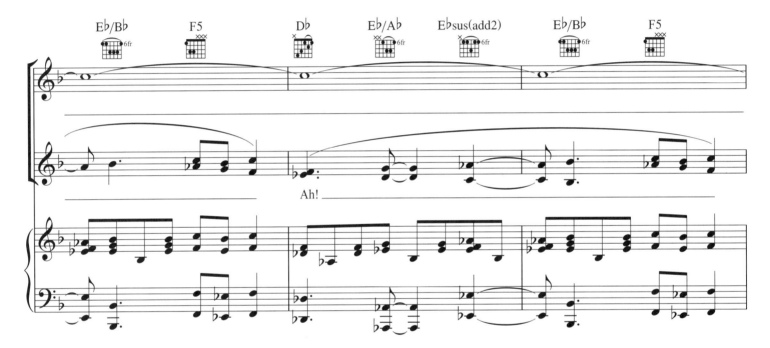

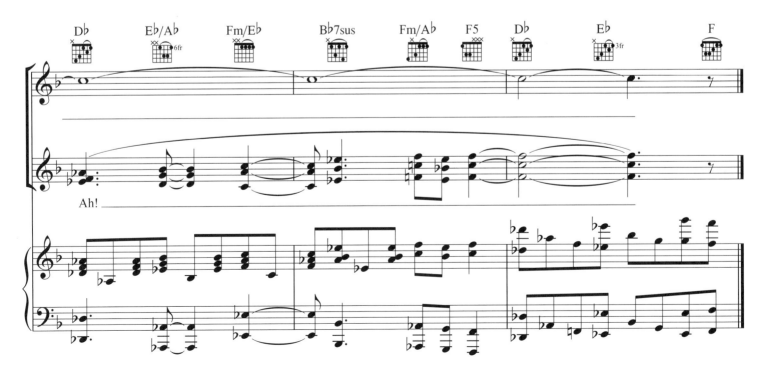

DEEP LOVE
from YOUNG FRANKENSTEIN

Music and Lyrics by
MEL BROOKS

ELIZABETH: *Penny for your thoughts. You know, until now my life has been nothing but a meaningless whirl of silly parties. But I always sensed that something was missing.*

Love! And I'm not talking about puppy love, either, one-night stand love or cheap love. No!

What I'm talkin' about is... what's the word I'm looking for?... Oh, yes...

PART OF YOUR WORLD

from Walt Disney's THE LITTLE MERMAID - A BROADWAY MUSICAL

Music by ALAN MENKEN
Lyrics by HOWARD ASHMAN

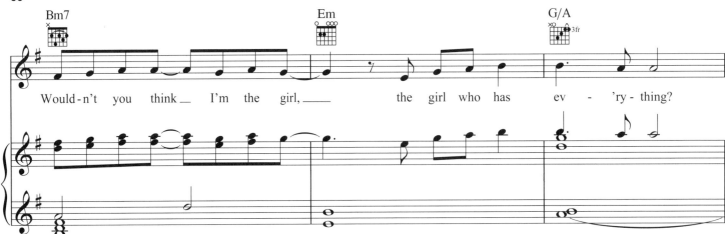

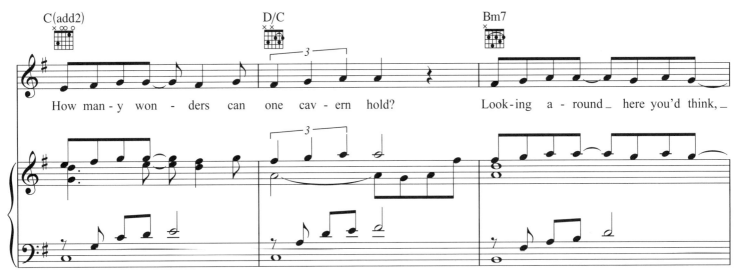

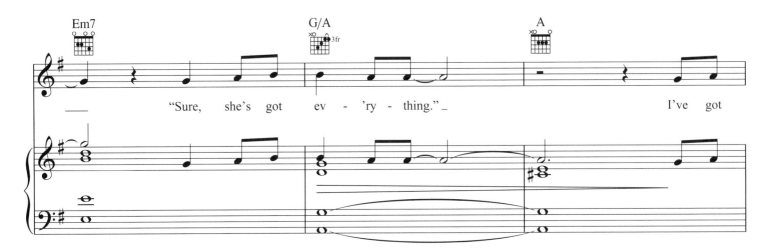

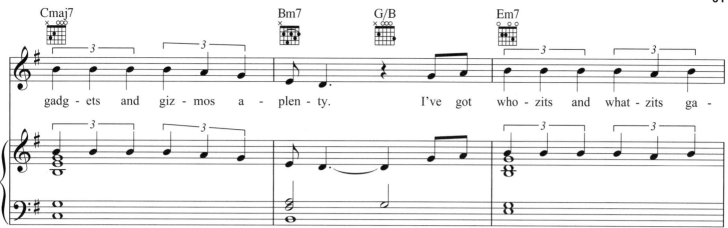

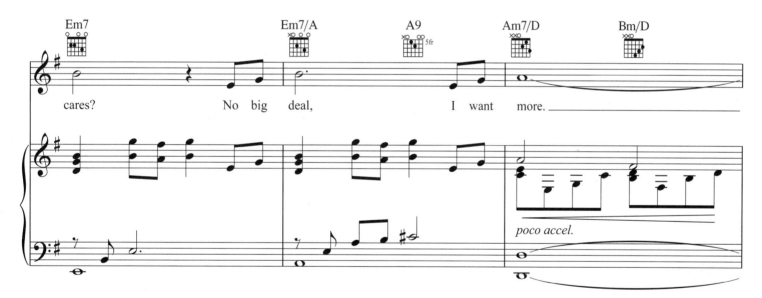

plore that shore up a - bove? Out of the

Freely

sea, wish I could be

part of that world.

IT WON'T BE LONG NOW

from IN THE HEIGHTS

Music and Lyrics by LIN-MANUEL MIRANDA
Arrangement by ALEX LACAMOIRE
and BILL SHERMAN

Allegro

p

With pedal

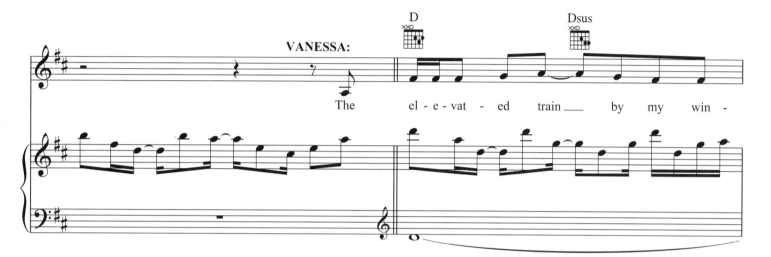

VANESSA:

The el-e-vat-ed train ___ by my win-

dow does-n't faze ___ me an-y-more. ___

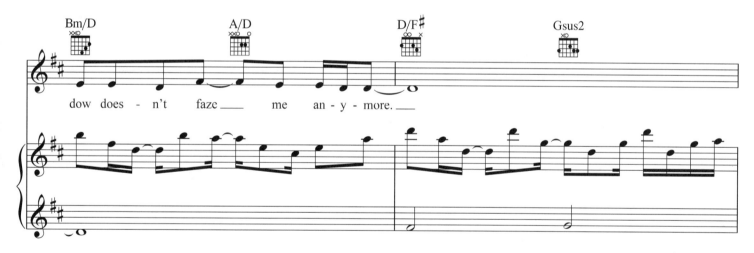

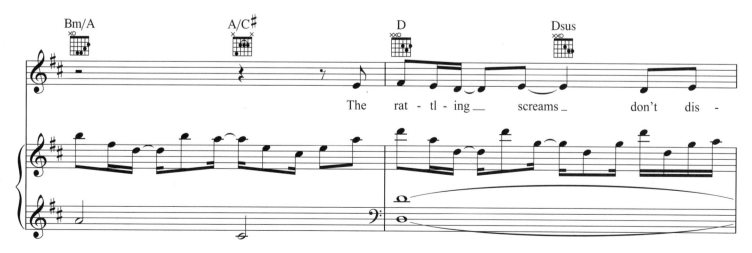

The rat-tl-ing ___ screams ___ don't dis-

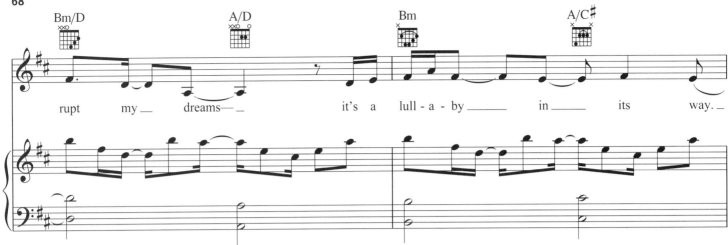

rupt my __ dreams___ __ it's a lull-a-by _____ in ____ its way. __

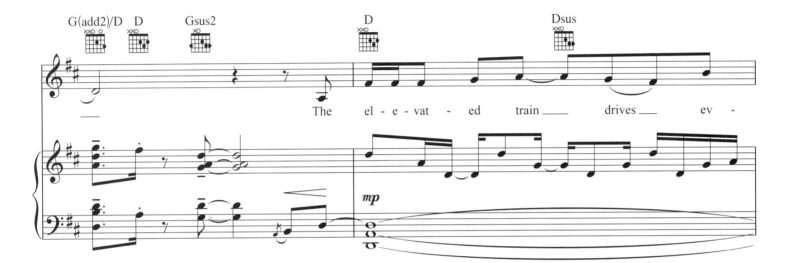

__ The el-e-vat-ed train ____ drives ____ ev-

'ry - one in - sane ___ but ___ I ____ don't ____ mind, ___ oh ____ no.

When I bring back_ boys, ___ they can't

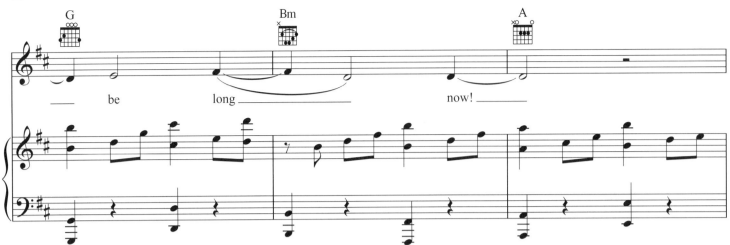

be long _____ now! _____

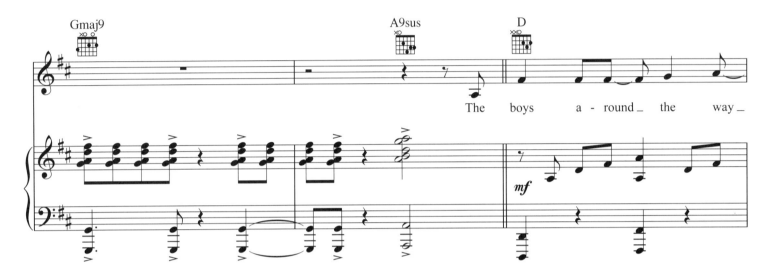

The boys a - round ___ the way ___

_____ hol - ler at me when I'm walk - ing down the street. _____

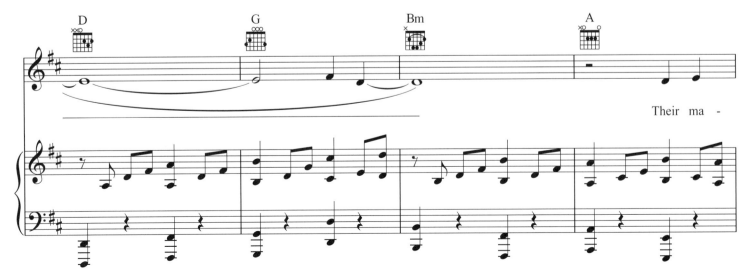

Their ma -

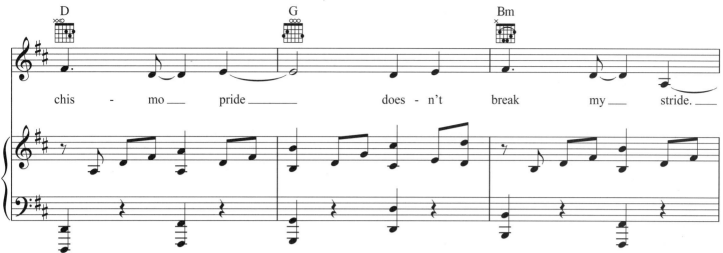

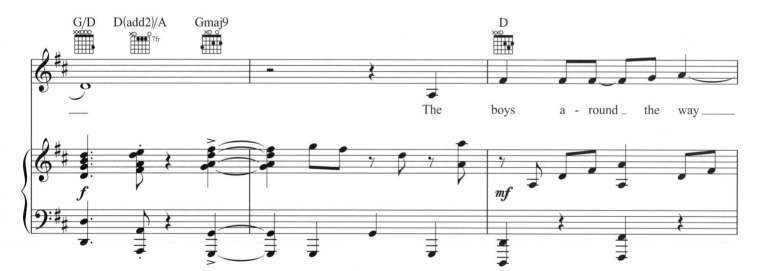

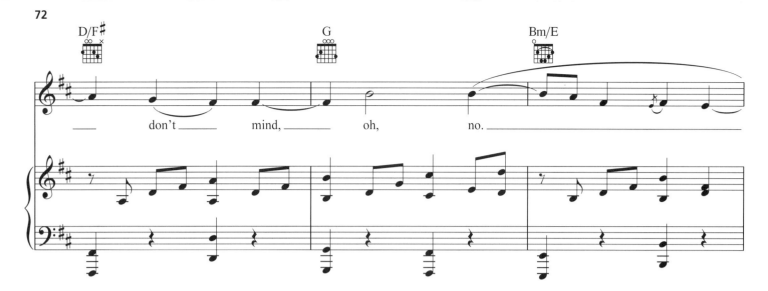

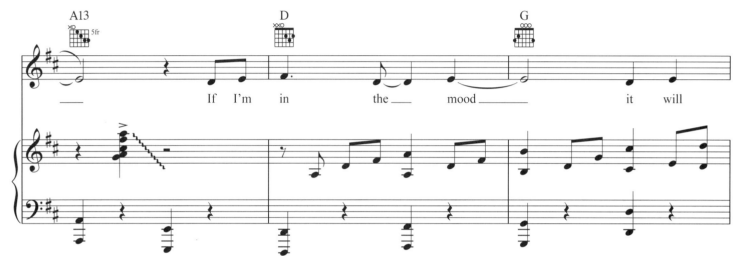

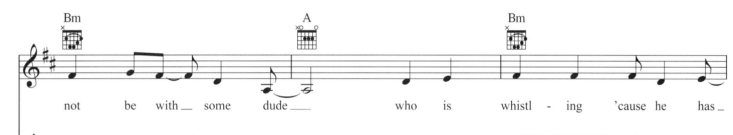

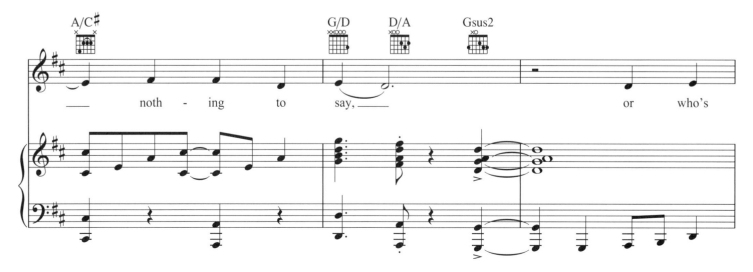

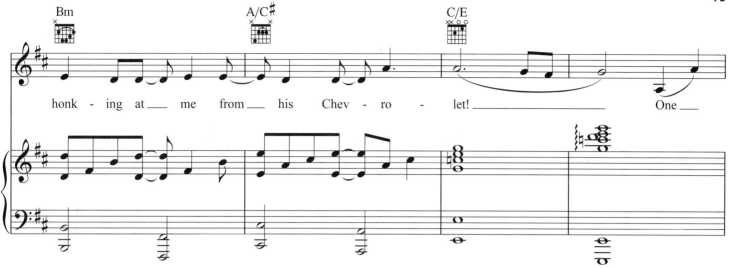

honk - ing at __ me from __ his Chev - ro - let! _____ One __

day, I'm hop - pin' in a lim - ou - sine __ and I'm driv -

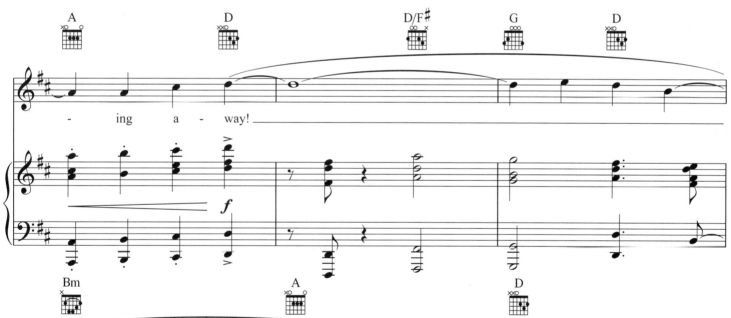

- ing a - way! _____

It won't __

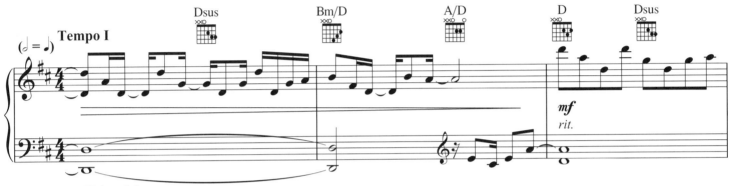

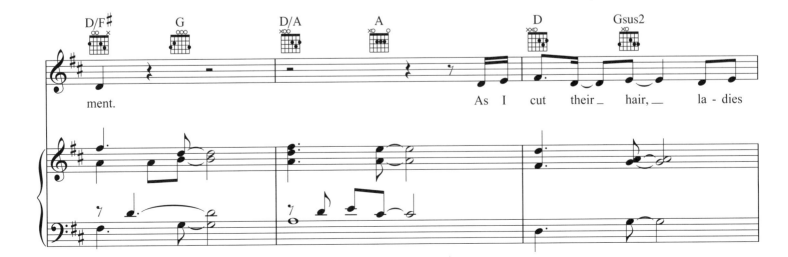

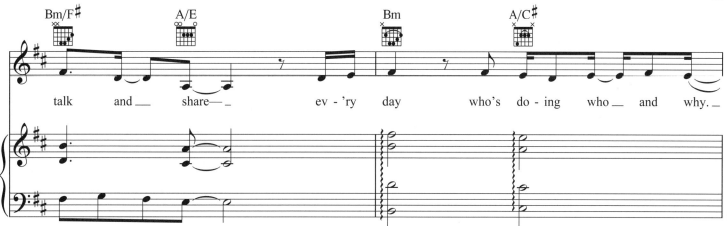

talk and __ share __ ev-'ry day who's do-ing who __ and why. __

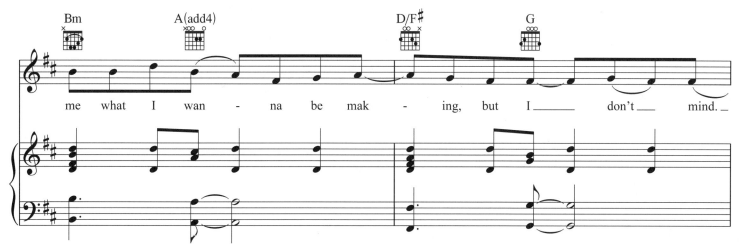

In tempo

The neigh-bor-hood sa-lon __ does-n't pay

me what I wan-na be mak-ing, but I ___ don't __ mind. __

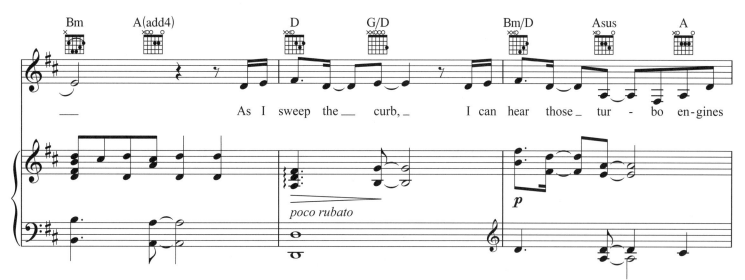

__ As I sweep the __ curb, __ I can hear those __ tur-bo en-gines

WHAT IT MEANS TO BE A FRIEND

from the Broadway Musical 13

Music and Lyrics by
JASON ROBERT BROWN

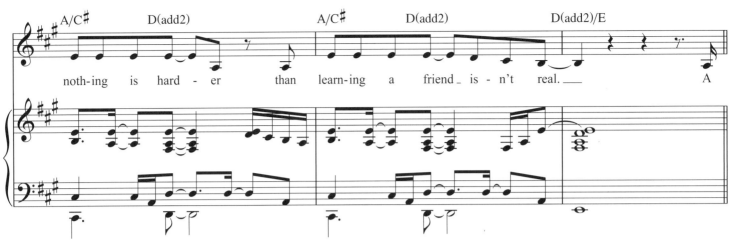

noth-ing is hard-er than learn-ing a friend is-n't real. ___ A

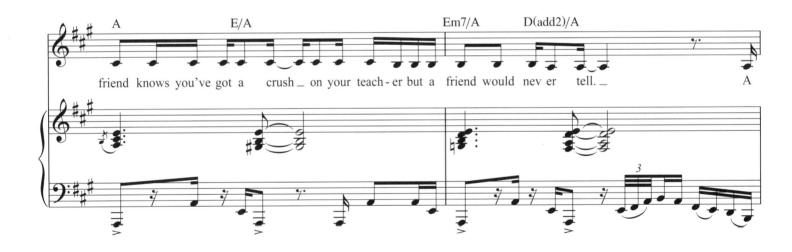

friend sends notes back and forth all day _ and does-n't care that you _ can't spell. _ A

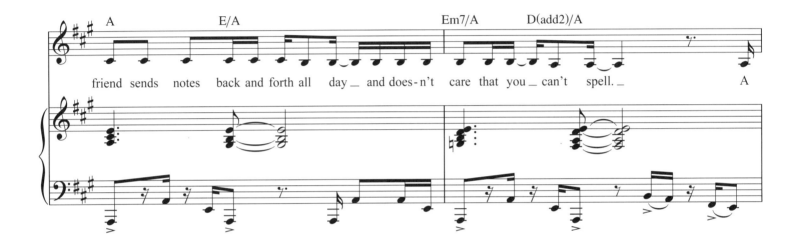

friend knows you've got a crush _ on your teach-er but a friend would nev-er tell. _ A

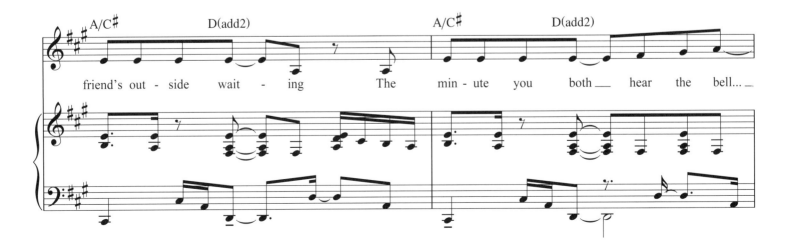

friend's out-side wait-ing The min-ute you both __ hear the bell... _

And if your heart _____ is al - ways break -

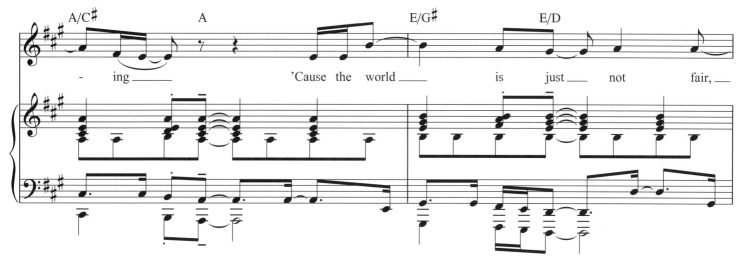

- ing _____ 'Cause the world _____ is just _ not fair, _

When you're at _____ your worst, _ Your friend's _ the first _ one there, _

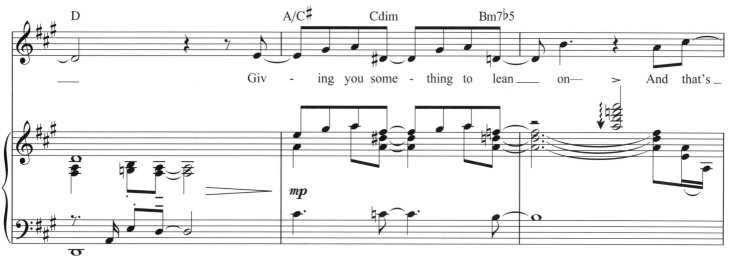

Giv - ing you some - thing to lean _ on— And that's _

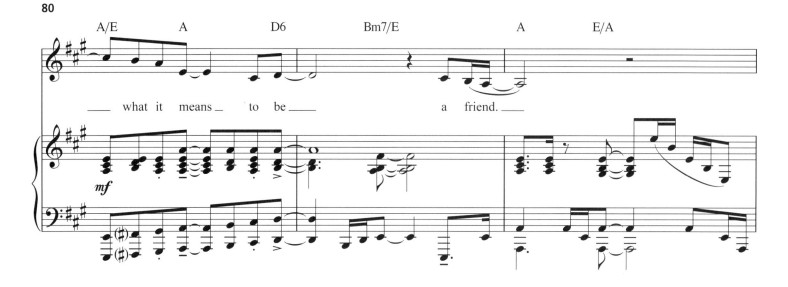

what it means___ to be___ a friend.___

friend won't smoke when she's in your room___ Or laugh at the po-ems you write.

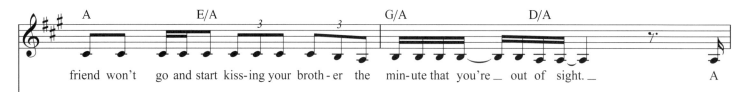

friend won't go and start kiss-ing your broth-er the min-ute that you're___ out of sight.___

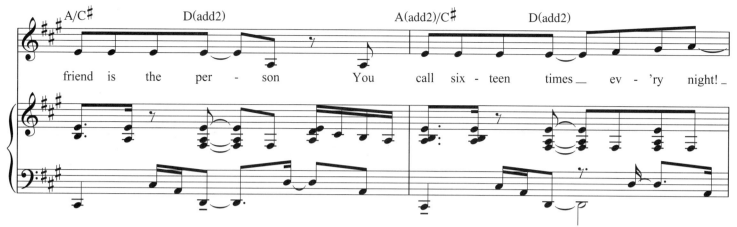

friend is the per - son You call six - teen times ___ ev - 'ry night! ___

___ And if your heart ___ is al - ways break - ing, ___ And you want ___

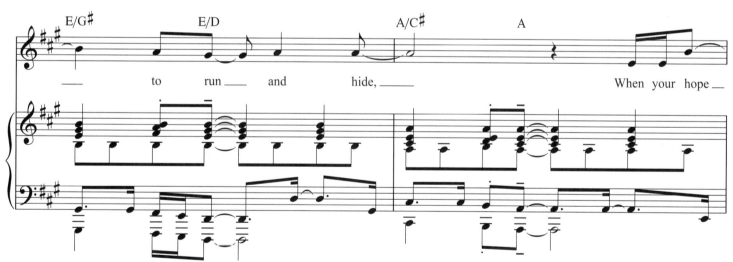

___ to run ___ and hide, ___ When your hope ___

___ is gone, ___ Your friend ___ is on ___ your side. ___ If some -

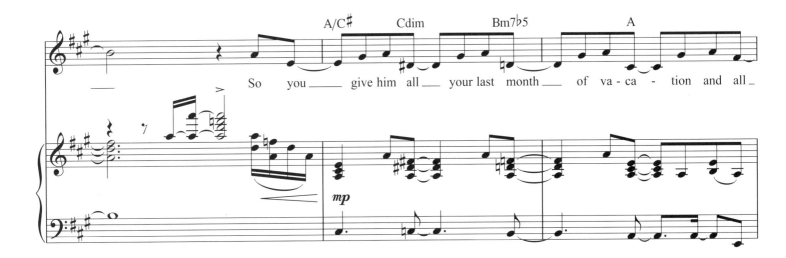

ELECTRICITY
from the Broadway Musical BILLY ELLIOT

Music by ELTON JOHN
Lyrics by LEE HALL

pose it's like for - get - ting, los - ing who you are, ___ and at the
like when you've been cry - ing, and you're emp - ty, and you're full, ___ but I

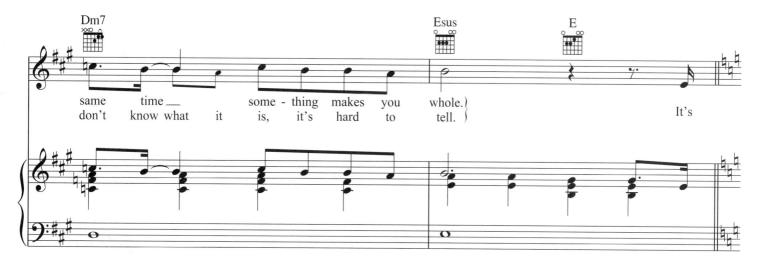

same time ___ some - thing makes you whole.} It's
don't know what it is, it's hard to tell.}

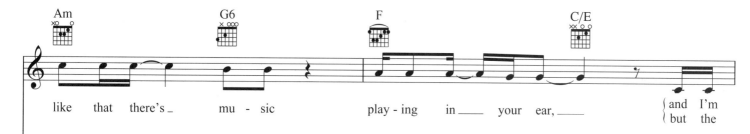

like that there's ___ mu - sic play - ing in ___ your ear, ___ {and I'm
{but the

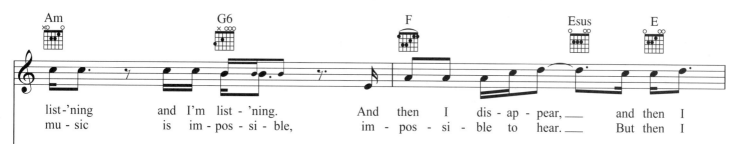

list - 'ning and I'm list - 'ning. And then I dis - ap - pear, ___ and then I
mu - sic is im - pos - si - ble, im - pos - si - ble to hear. ___ But then I

I KNOW IT'S TODAY

from SHREK THE MUSICAL

Words and Music by DAVID LINDSEY-ABAIRE
and JEANINE TESORI

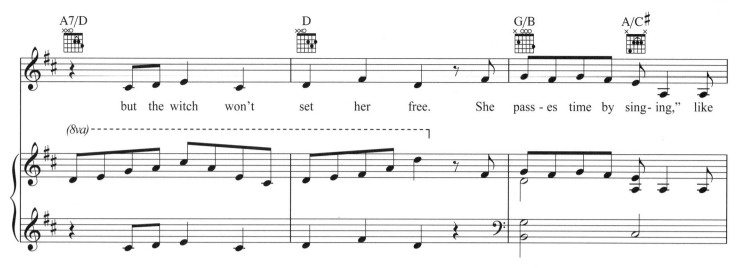

but the witch won't set her free. She pass-es time by sing-ing," like

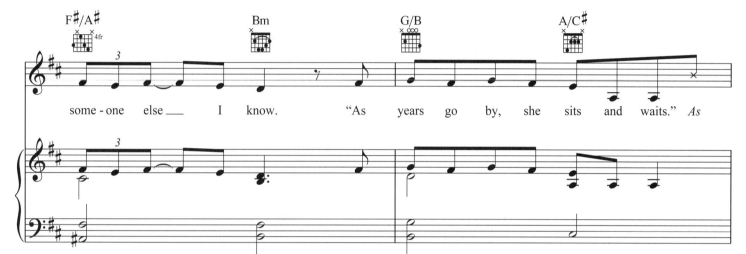

some-one else ___ I know. "As years go by, she sits and waits." As

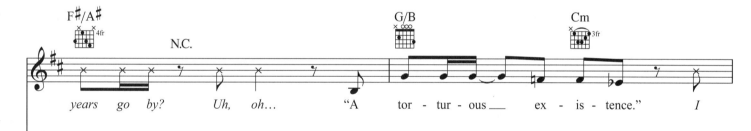

years go by? Uh, oh... "A tor-tur-ous ___ ex-is-tence." I

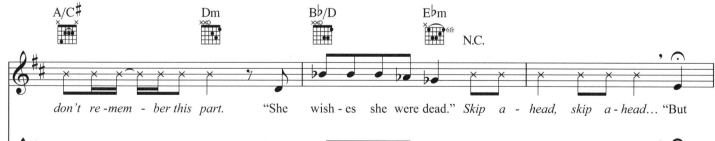

don't re-mem-ber this part. "She wish-es she were dead." Skip a-head, skip a-head... "But

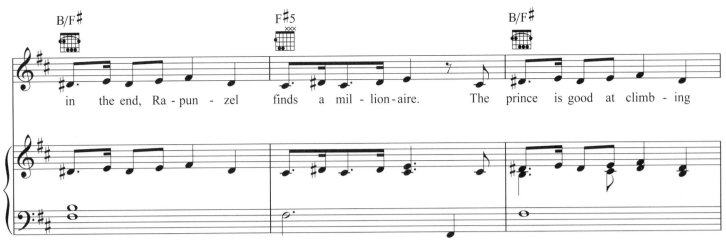

in the end, Ra - pun - zel finds a mil - lion - aire. The prince is good at climb - ing

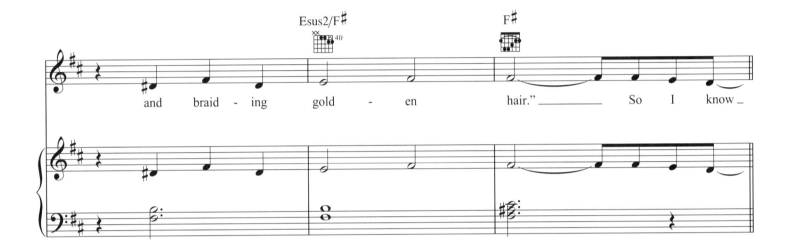

and braid - ing gold - en hair." _____ So I know _

_ he'll ap - pear _____ 'cause there are rules and there _ are stric -

- tures. _ I be - lieve the sto - ry - books _ I read _

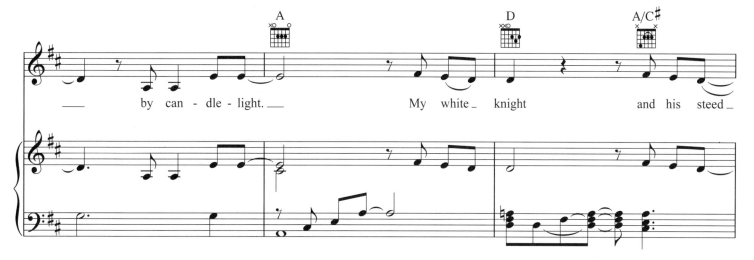

by can - dle - light. ___ My white ___ knight ___ and his steed ___

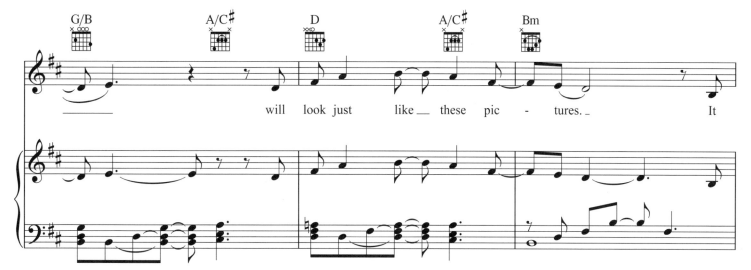

___ will look just like ___ these pic - tures. ___ It

won't be ___ long ___ now, I guar - an - tee. ___

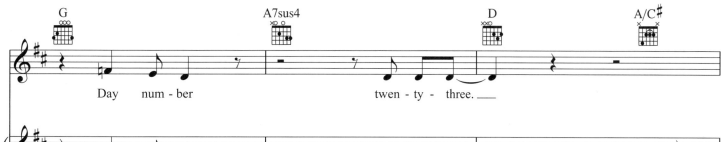

Day num - ber twen - ty - three. ___

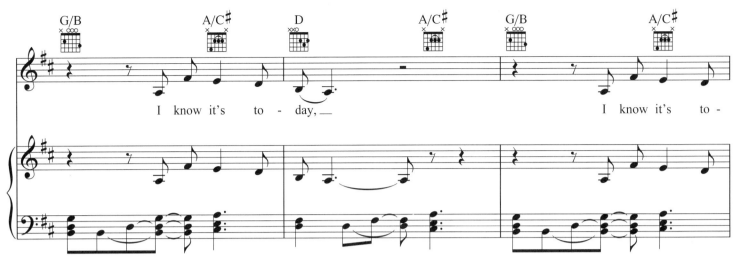

I know it's to - day, ___ I know it's to -

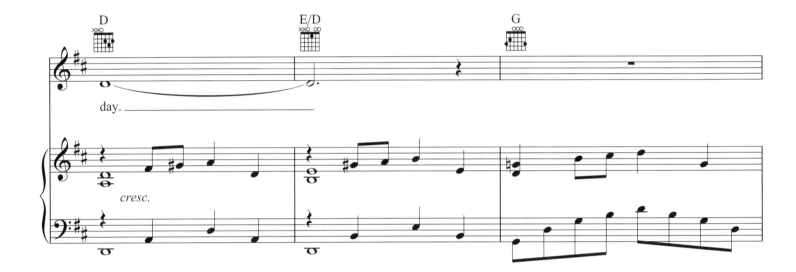

day. ___

cresc.

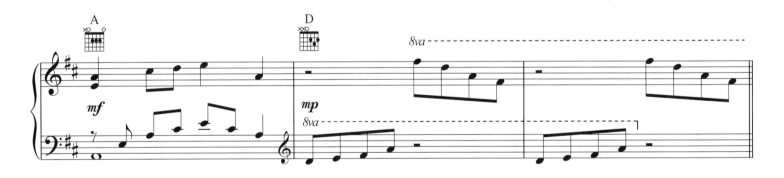

mf *mp*

8va

8va

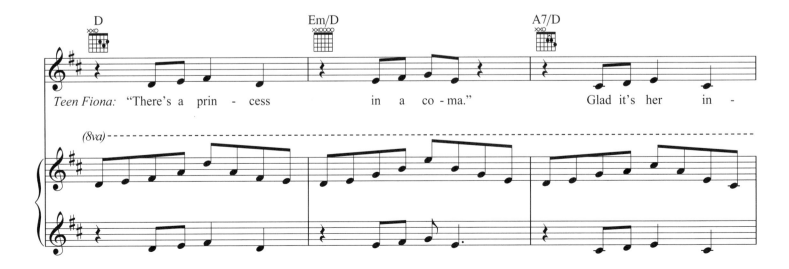

Teen Fiona: "There's a prin - cess in a co - ma." Glad it's her in -

(8va)

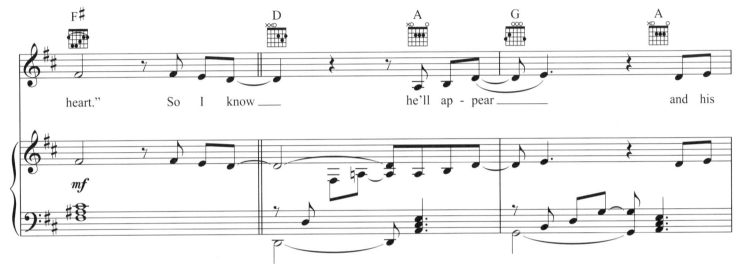

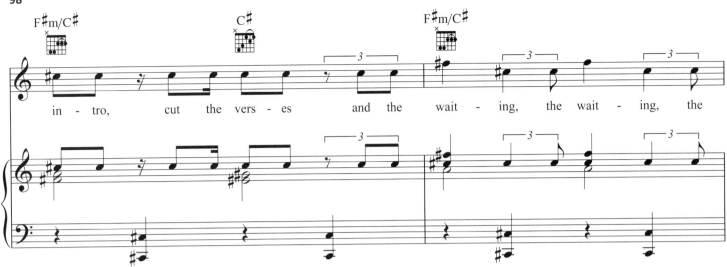

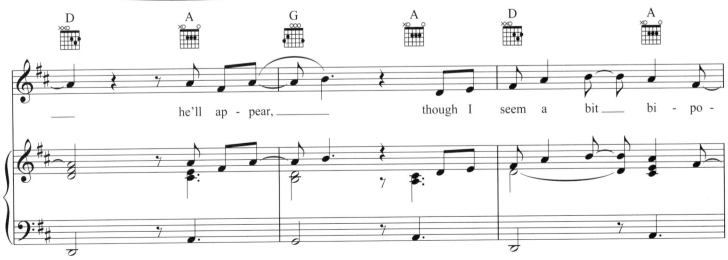

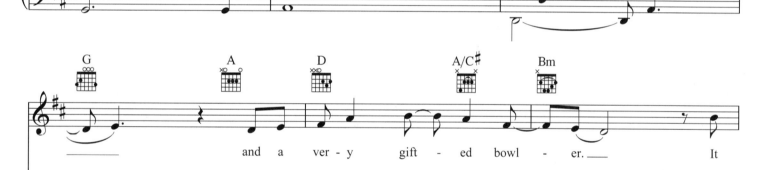

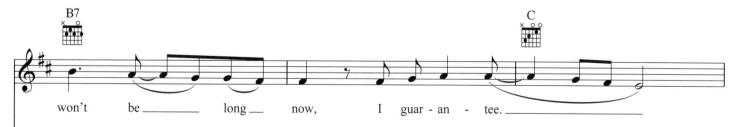

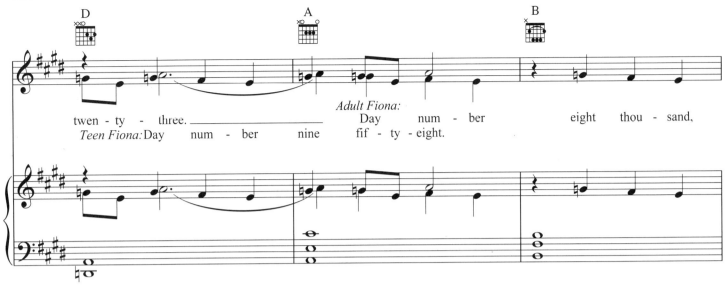

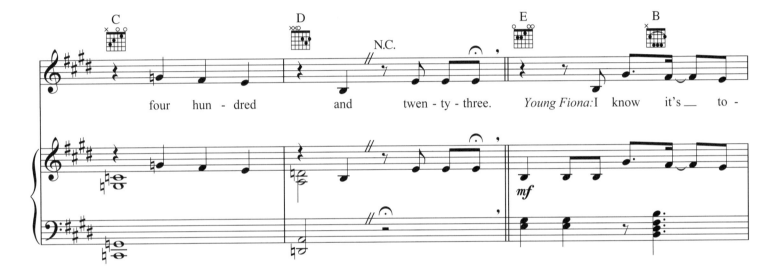

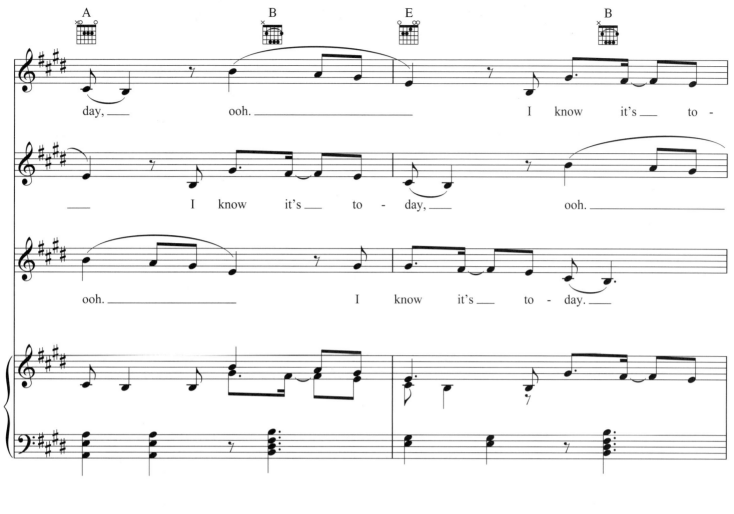

WE BUILT THIS CITY
from ROCK OF AGES

Words and Music by BERNIE TAUPIN,
MARTIN PAGE, DENNIS LAMBERT
and PETER WOLF

Medium Rock

We built this cit - y, we built this cit - y on

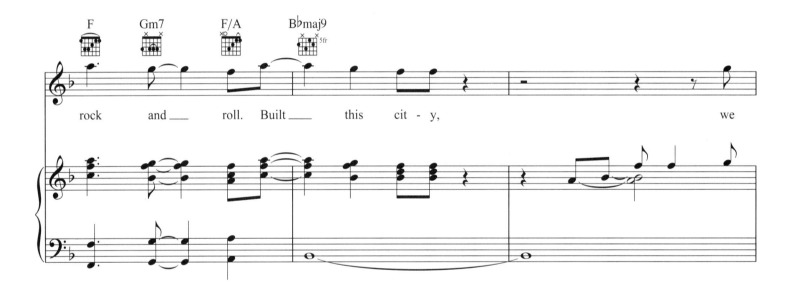

rock and ___ roll. Built ___ this cit - y, we

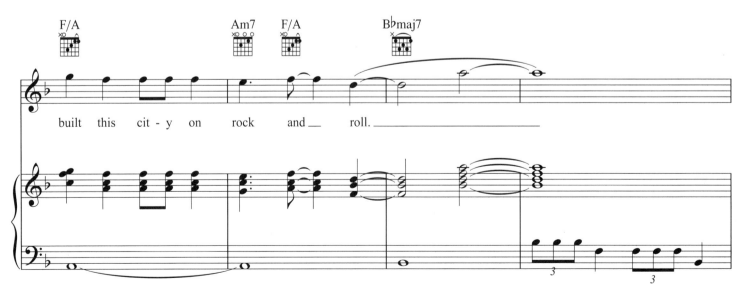

built this cit - y on rock and ___ roll. _____

With a driving beat

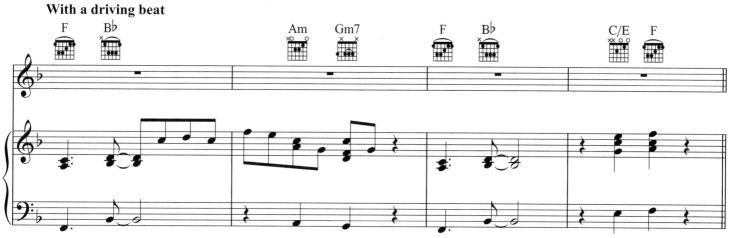

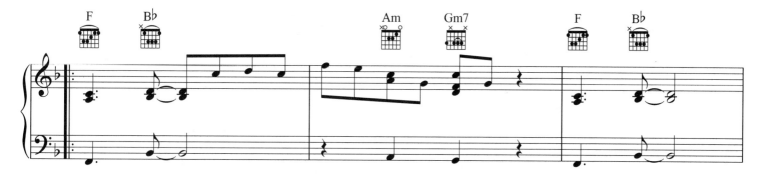

Say _____ you don't know me or rec-o-
Some - one al - ways play - ing cor-
_____ counts the mon - ey un -

- og - nize my face.
- por - a - tion games.
- der-neath the bar?

Say _____ you don't care who goes _____
Who _____ cares, they're al - ways chang -
Who rides the wreck - ing ball _____

to that ___ kind of place.
- ing   cor - por - a - tion names. ___
in two ___ rock gui - tars?

Knee ___
We ___
Don't ___

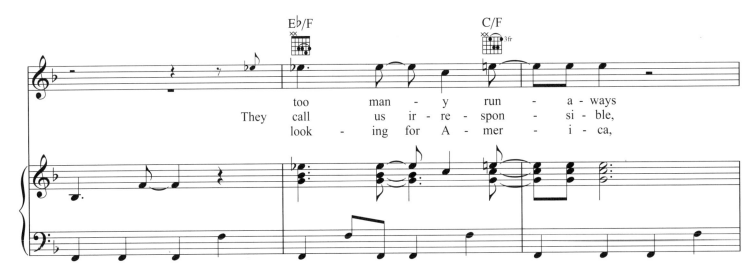

___ deep in the hoop - la,
___ just want to dance here,
___ tell us you need us,

sink - ing in your fight,
some - one stole the stage.
'cause we're ___ the ship of fools,

too man - y run - a - ways
They call us ir - re - spon - si - ble,
look - ing for A - mer - i - ca,

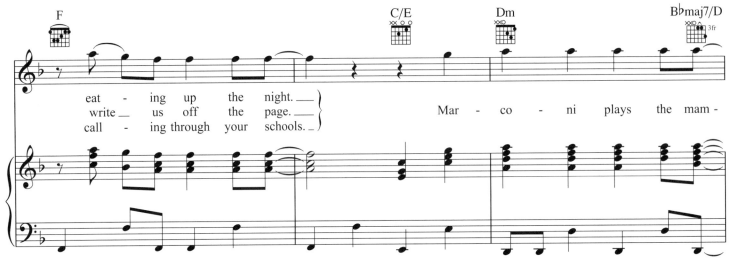

eat - ing up the night. ___
write ___ us off the page. ___
call - ing through your schools. ___

Mar - co - ni plays the mam -

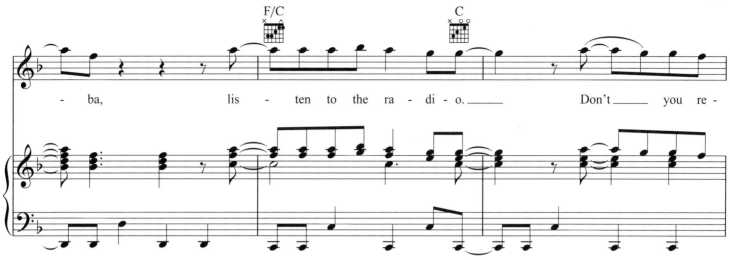

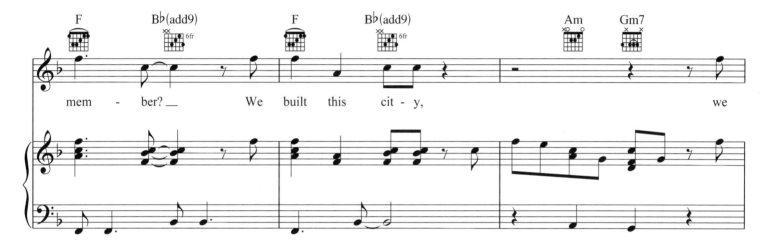

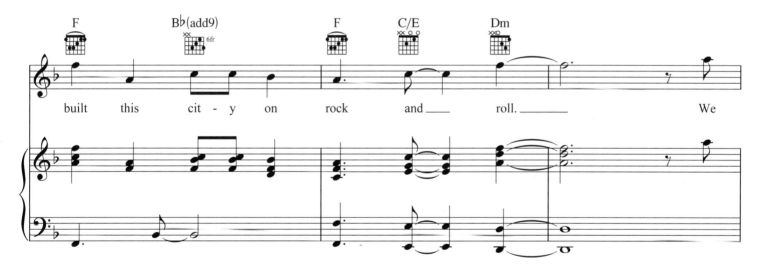

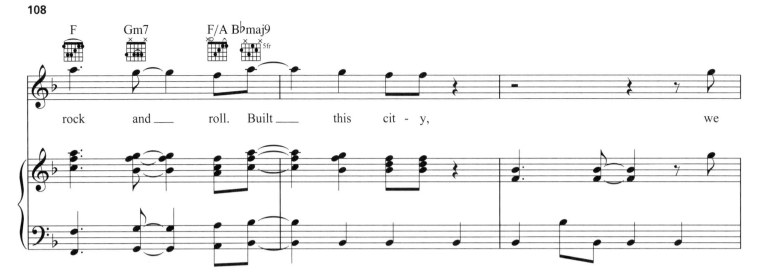

rock and ___ roll. Built ___ this cit - y, we

built this cit - y on rock and ___ roll. ___

To Coda

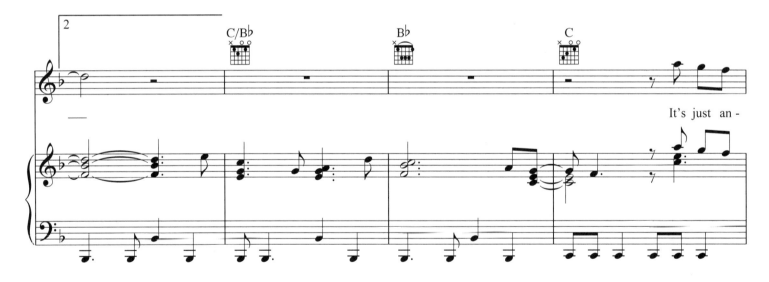

It's just an -

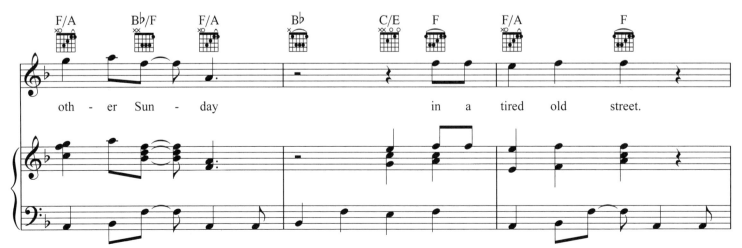

oth - er Sun - day   in a tired old street.

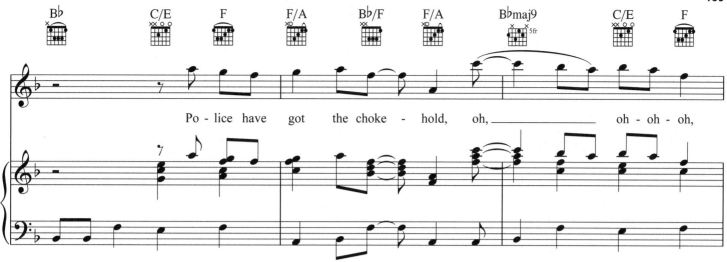

Po - lice have got the choke - hold, oh, _____ oh - oh - oh,

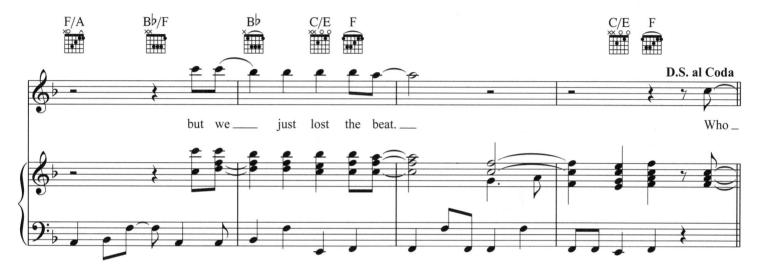

D.S. al Coda

but we ___ just lost the beat. ___ Who ___

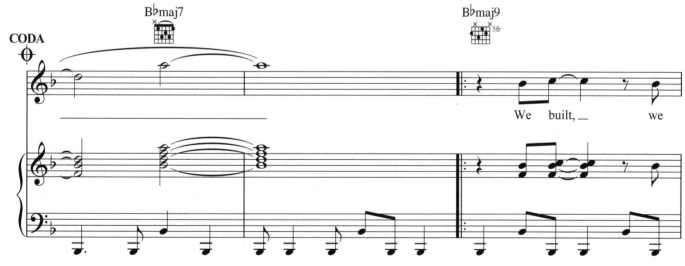

CODA

We built, ___ we

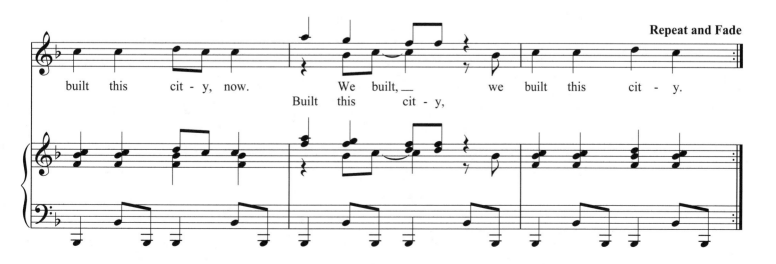

Repeat and Fade

built this cit - y, now. We built, ___ we built this cit - y.
Built this cit - y,

I'M ALIVE
from NEXT TO NORMAL

Lyrics by BRIAN YORKEY
Music by TOM KITT

Moderately bright rock ♩ = 160

(High-hat)

Rhythmic Guitar progression

Gabe:

I am what you want___ me to be, and I'm your___ worst fear,___ you'll find___ it in me.___ Come clos - er... Come

clos - er...   I am more than mem-

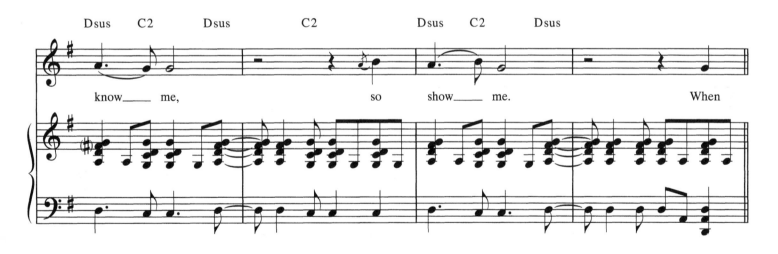

o - ry,   I am what___ might be,   I am mys - ter - y.   You

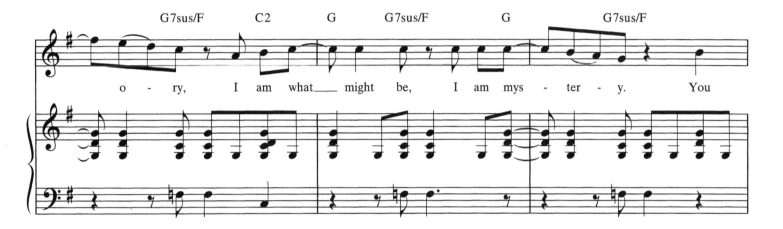

know___ me,   so   show___ me.   When

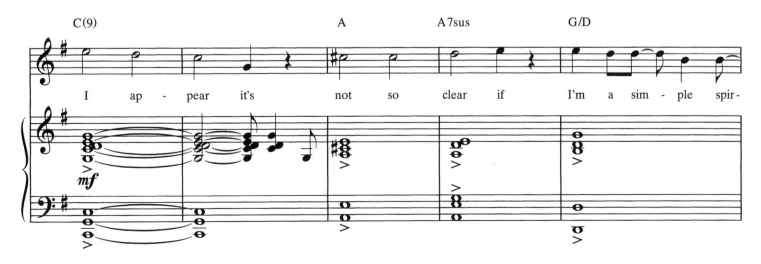

I ap - pear   it's   not so   clear   if   I'm a sim - ple spir-

Bouncy

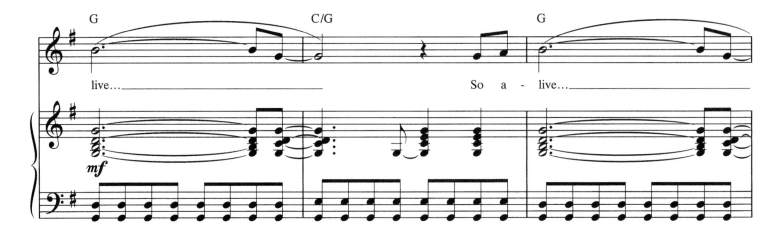

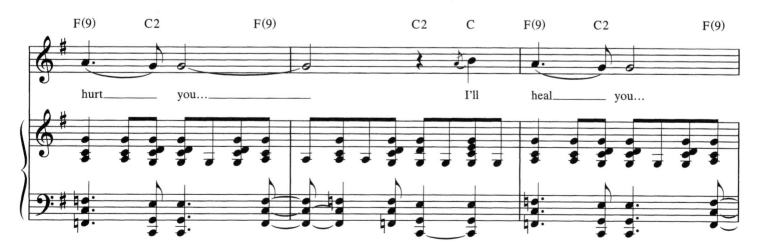

change me. I'm the per-fect strang-er who__ knows you__

Tempo I

__ too well._____ And I'm a-live,__ I'm a-live, I am

so a-live, and I'll tell you the truth__ if you let__ me try.__ You're a-

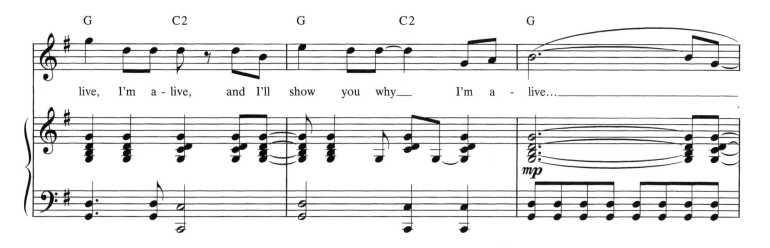

live, I'm a-live, and I'll show you why__ I'm a-live...._____

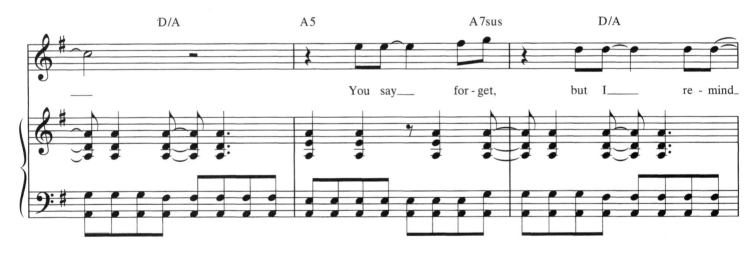

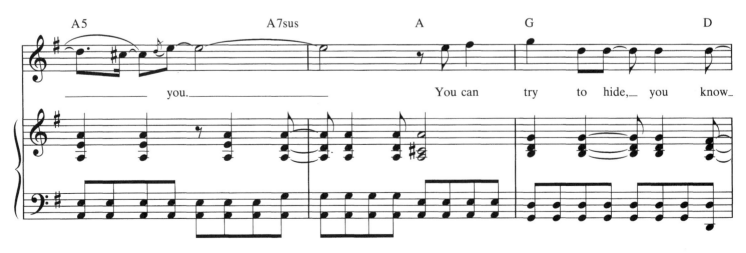

that I___ will find___ you._____ 'Cause if

you won't grieve_____ me, you won't

leave me be - hind..._____ Oh

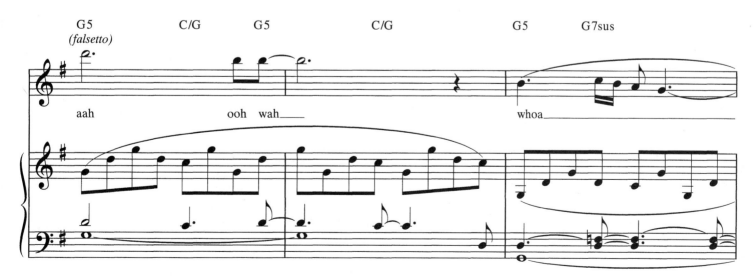

(falsetto)

aah ooh wah___ whoa_____

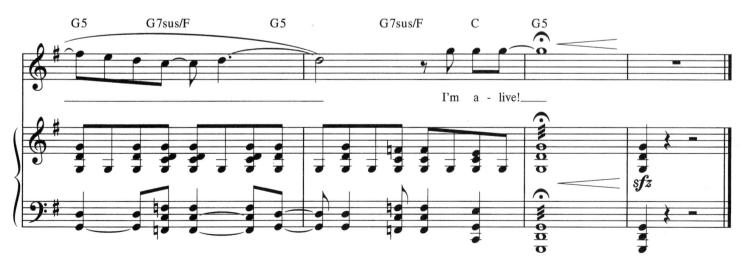

MEMPHIS LIVES IN ME

from MEMPHIS

Music by DAVID BRYAN
Lyrics by JOE DiPIETRO
and DAVID BRYAN

Medium slow Ballad

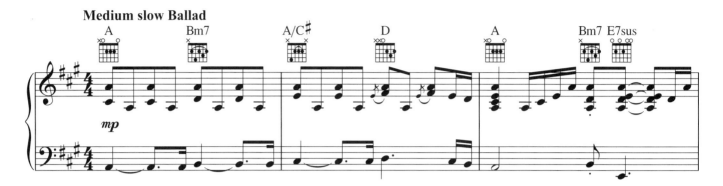

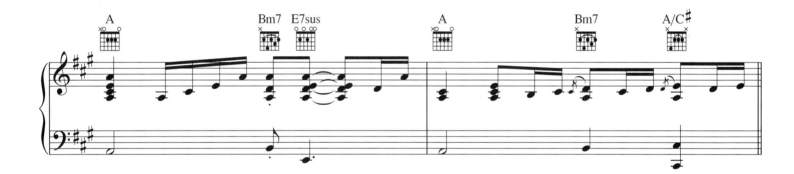

HUEY: There's a town that I ___ call home, ___ 3

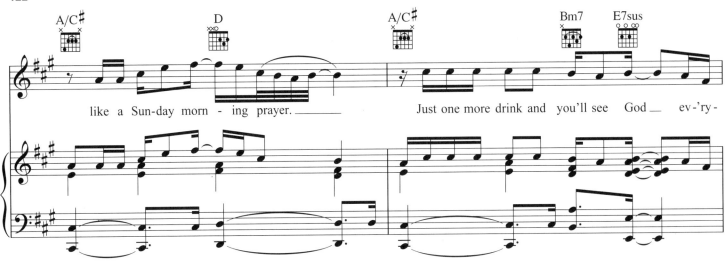

like a Sun-day morn - ing prayer.____ Just one more drink and you'll see God__ ev-'ry-

where. Like a sad old mel - o - dy,

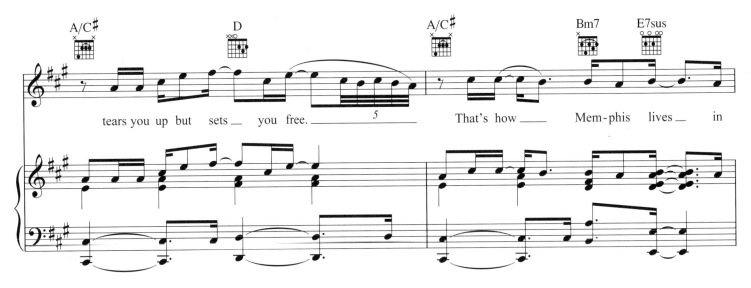

tears you up but sets__ you free.____ 5 That's how____ Mem-phis lives__ in

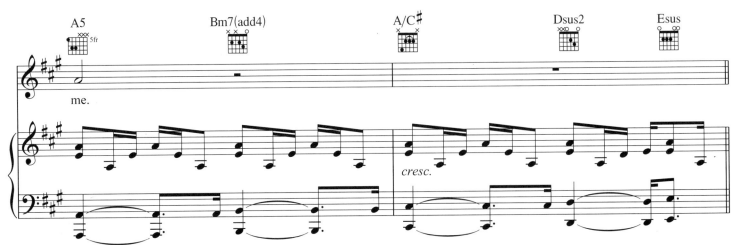

me.

cresc.

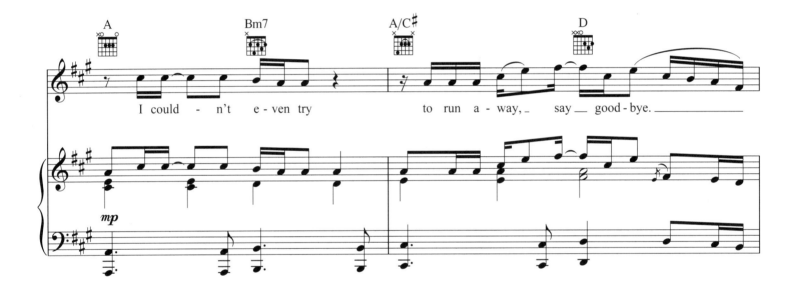

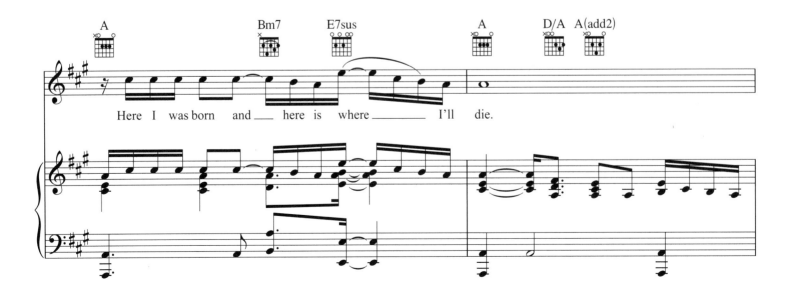

I'm just a man from ___ Ten-nes-see, ___ can't be ___ what ___ I ___ can't be. ___ *3*

All I know is Mem-phis lives ___ in me. ___ Whoa! ___

ENSEMBLE:

Oh _____ oh _____

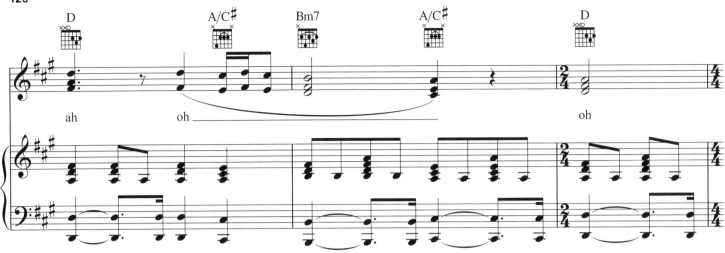

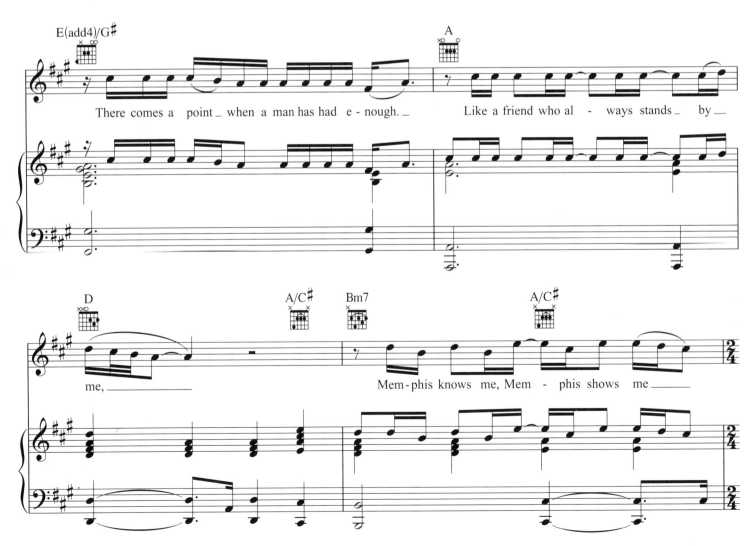

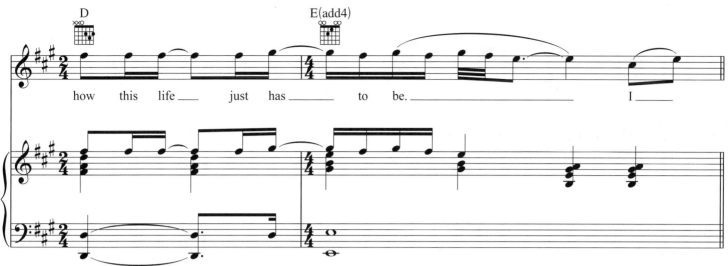

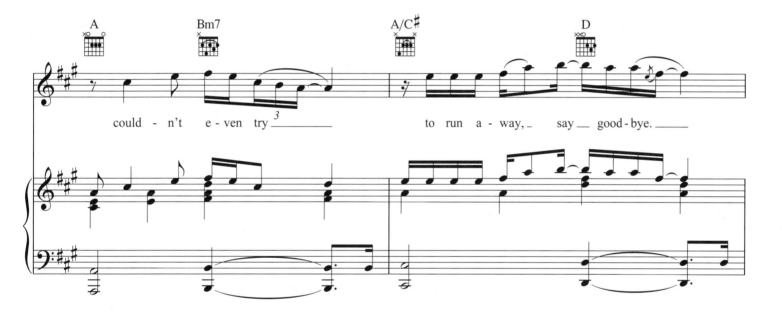

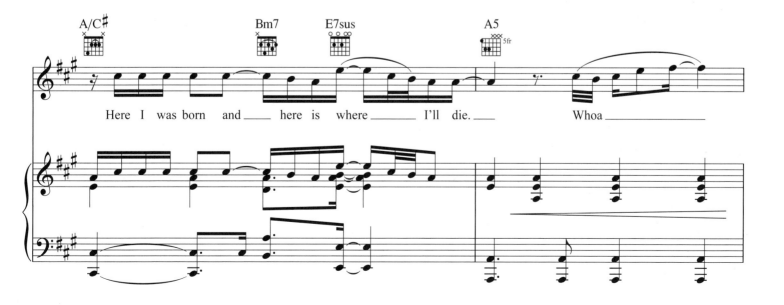

HAPPY/SAD
from THE ADDAMS FAMILY

Music and Lyrics by
ANDREW LIPPA

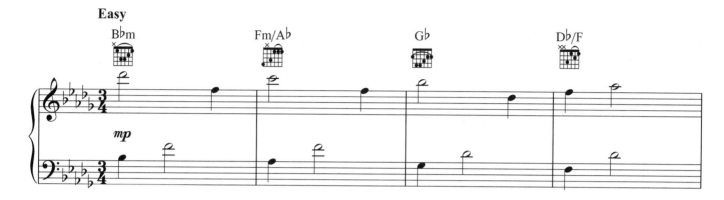

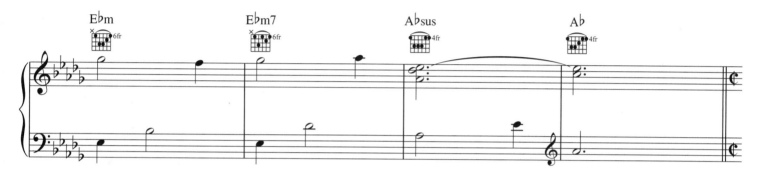

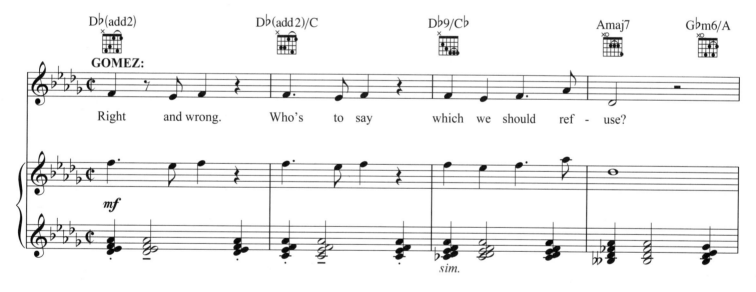

GOMEZ:

Right and wrong. Who's to say which we should ref - use?

All we know, love sur - vives, ei - ther way we choose.

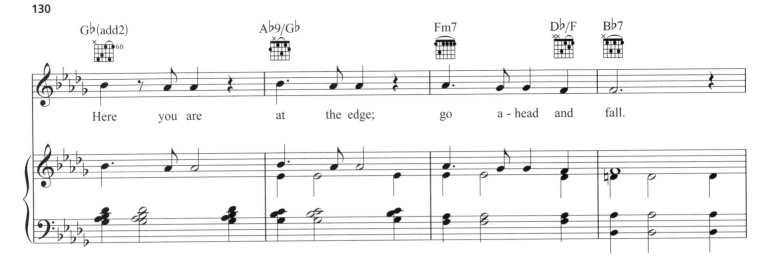

Here you are at the edge; go a-head and fall.

In 3, not too slow

Don't re-sist, I in-sist, love still con-quers all.

colla voce

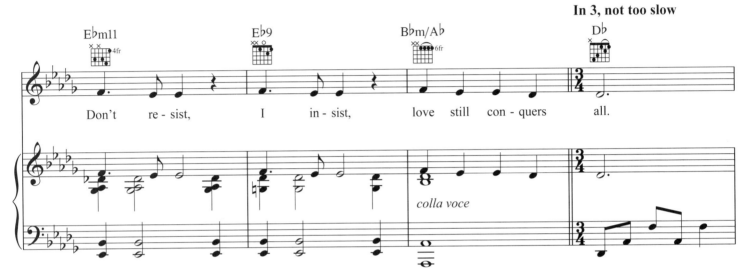

I'm feel-ing hap-py,

I'm feel-ing sad. A lit-tle child-ish,

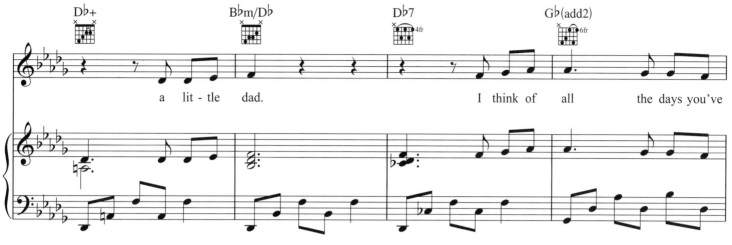

a lit - tle dad. I think of all the days you've

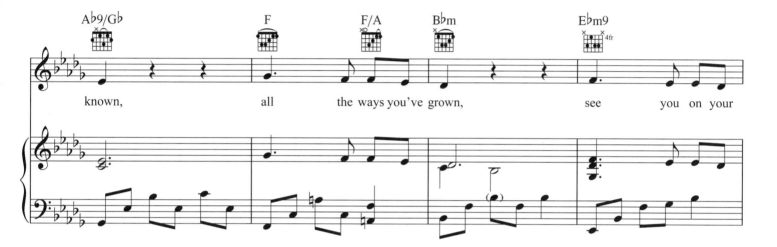

known, all the ways you've grown, see you on your

own, and then I'm feel - ing hap - py and

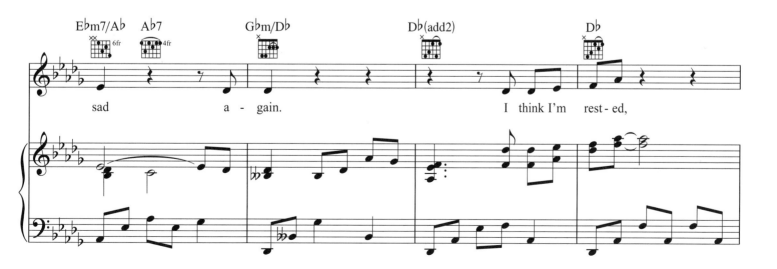

sad a - gain. I think I'm rest - ed,

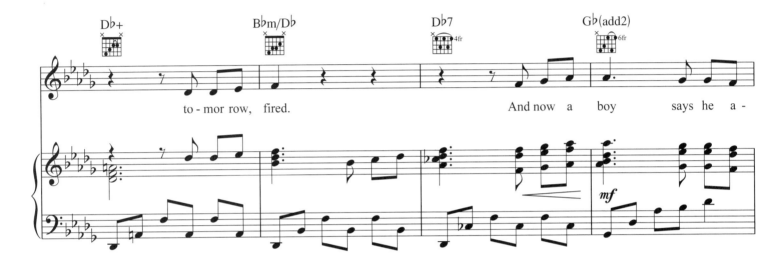

Why should I choose? Life is

full of con - tra - dic - tions, ev - 'ry

inch a mile. At the

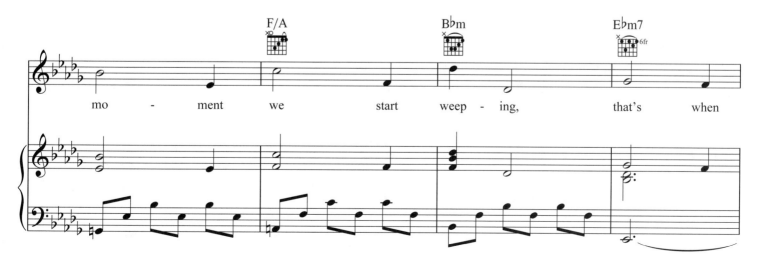

mo - ment we start weep - ing, that's when

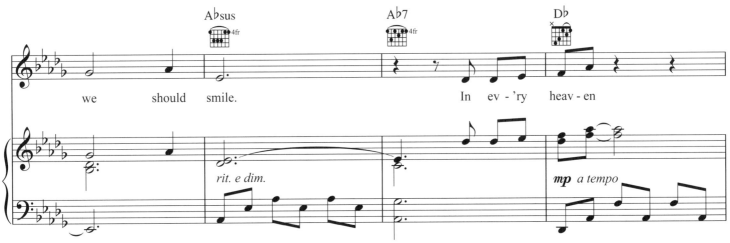

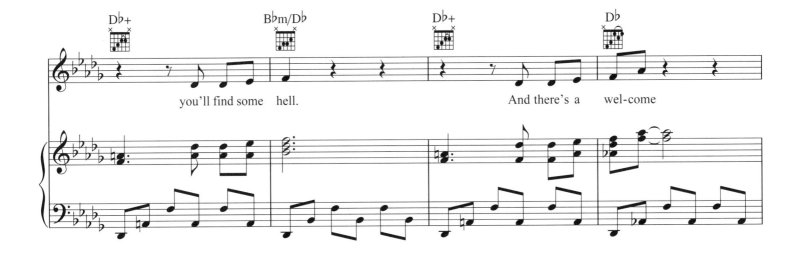

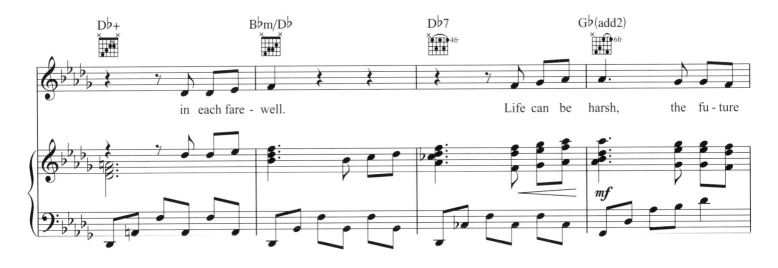

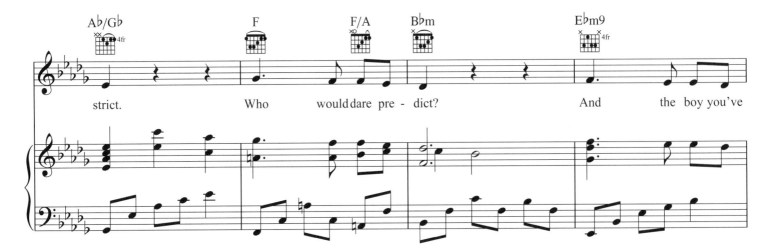

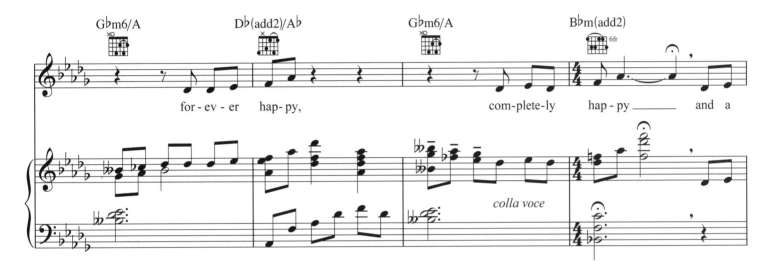

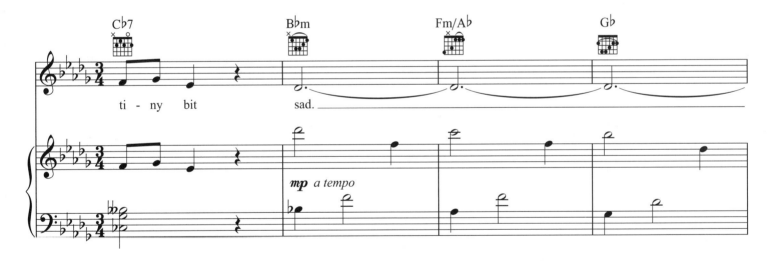

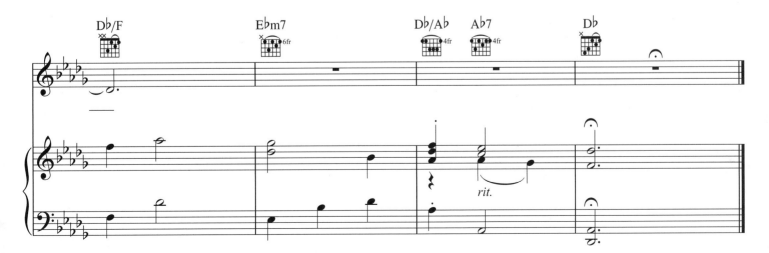

GREAT BALLS OF FIRE
from the Broadway Musical MILLION DOLLAR QUARTET

Words and Music by JACK HAMMER
and OTIS BLACKWELL

Bright Rock

You shake my nerves and you rat-tle my brain. _
Instrumental

Too much love drives a man in-sane. _ You broke my will,

but what a thrill. Good-ness gra-cious, great_ balls of fire!

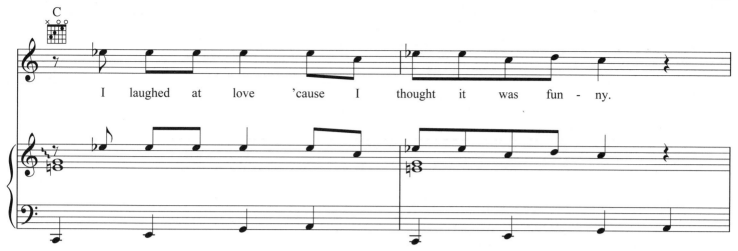

I laughed at love 'cause I thought it was fun - ny.

You came a - long and you moved __ me, hon - ey. I changed my mind,

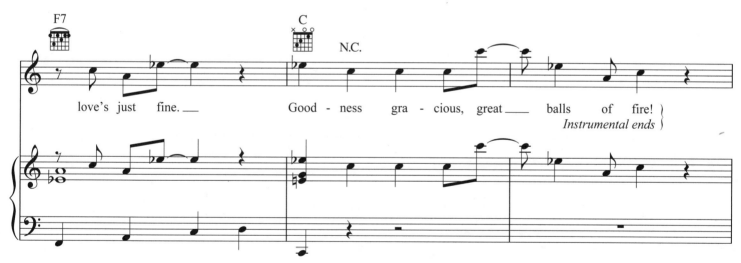

love's just fine. __ Good - ness gra - cious, great __ balls of fire!

Instrumental ends

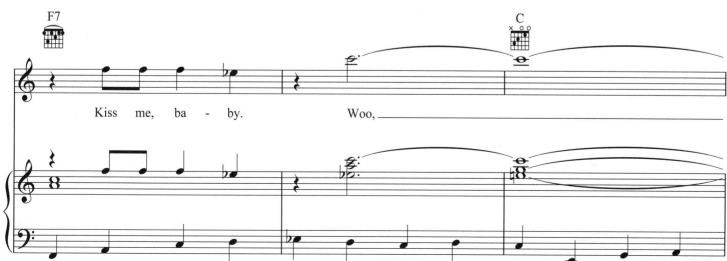

Kiss me, ba - by. Woo, __

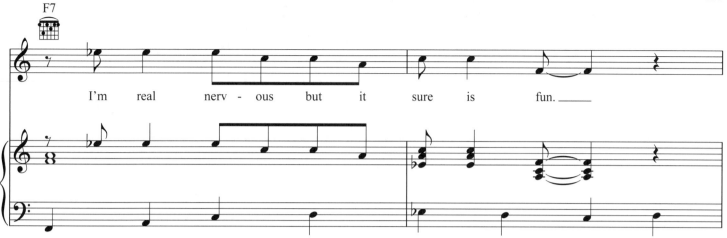

I'm real nerv - ous but it sure is fun. ____

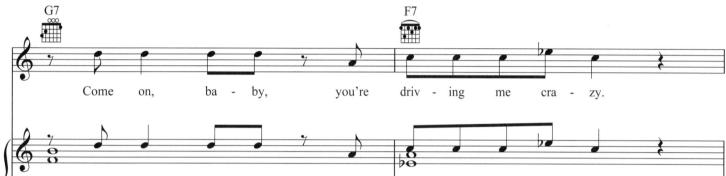

Come on, ba - by, you're driv - ing me cra - zy.

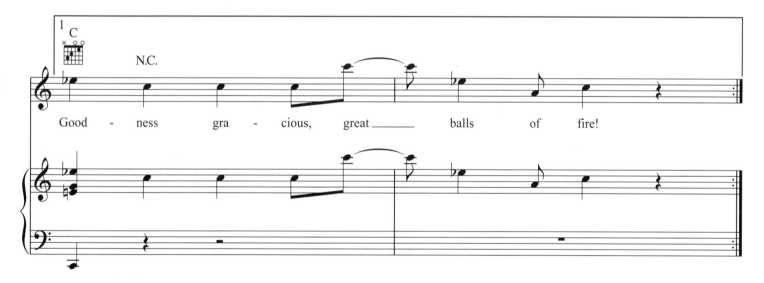

Good - ness gra - cious, great ____ balls of fire!

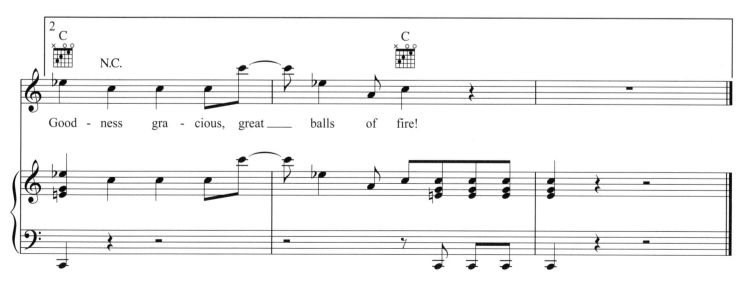

Good - ness gra - cious, great ____ balls of fire!

WAKE ME UP
WHEN SEPTEMBER ENDS

from the Broadway Musical AMERICAN IDIOT

Words by BILLIE JOE
Music by GREEN DAY

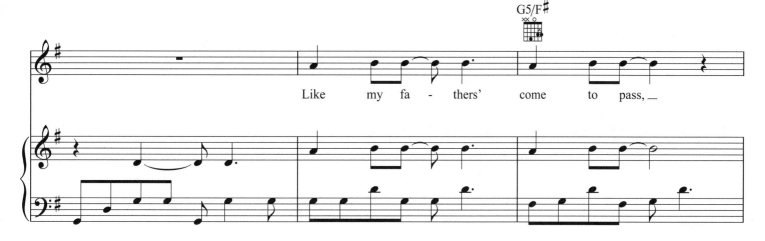

Like my fa - thers' come to pass, __

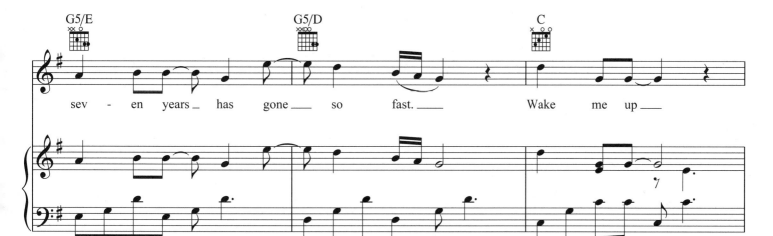

sev - en years __ has gone __ so fast. __ Wake me up __

when Sep-tem - ber ends. __ Here comes __ the

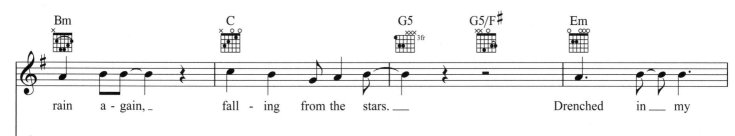

rain a - gain, __ fall - ing from the stars. __ Drenched in __ my

Drums enter

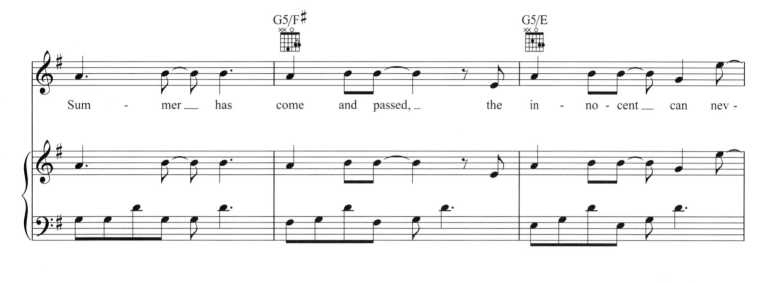

Sum - mer __ has come and passed, __ the in - no - cent __ can nev-

- er last. __ Wake me up __ when Sep - tem - ber ends. __

__ Ring out __ the

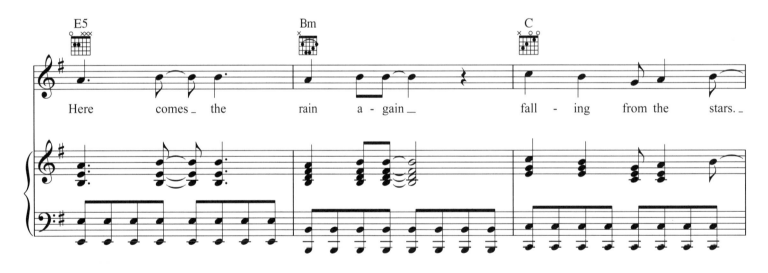

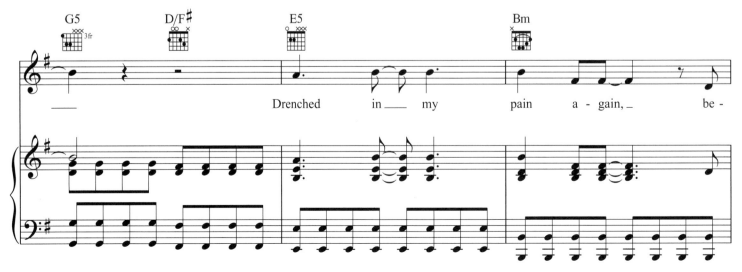

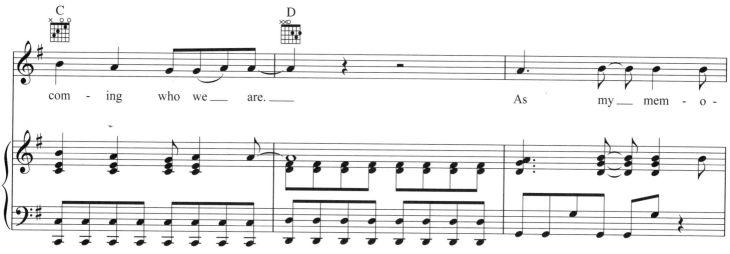

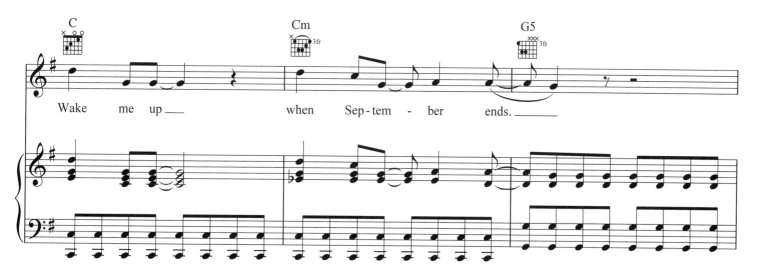

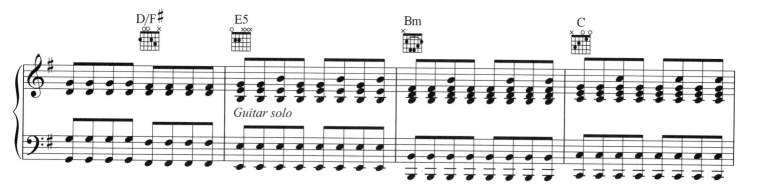

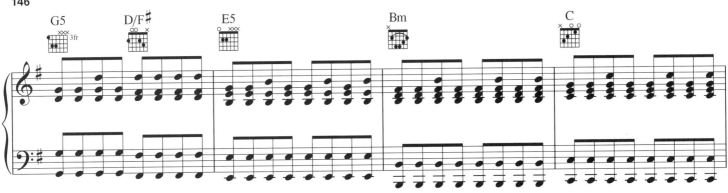

Sum - mer __ has come and passed, __ the in - no - cent __ can nev -

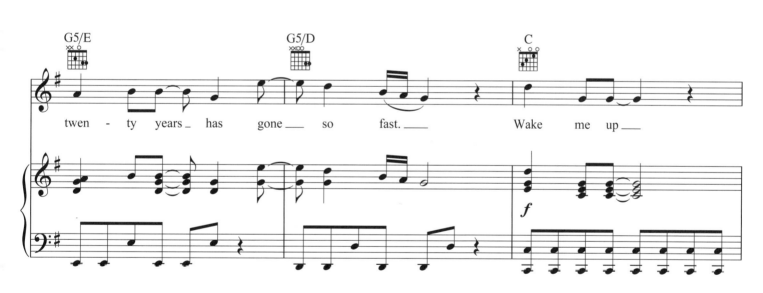

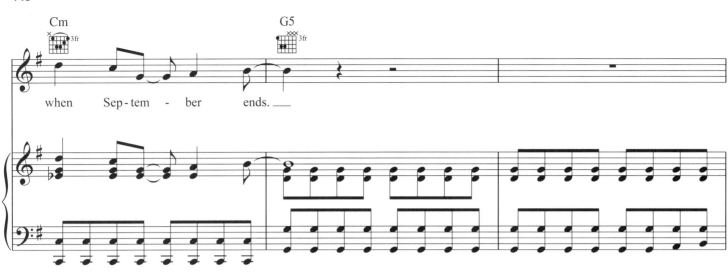

when Sep - tem - ber ends. ___

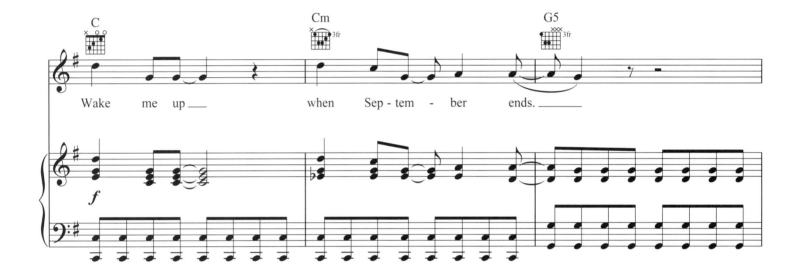

Wake me up ___ when Sep - tem - ber ends. _____

Freely

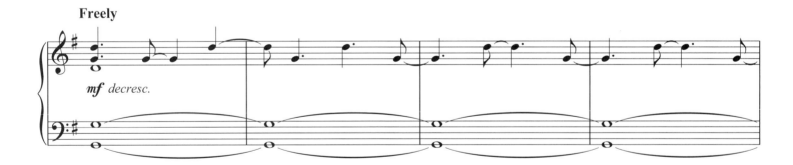

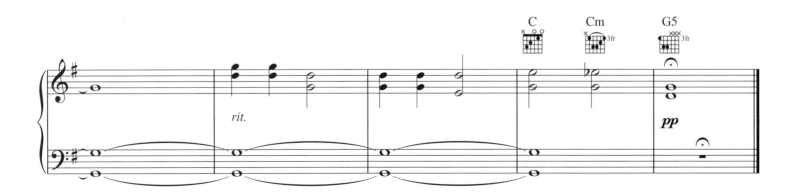

LET IT BE
from the Broadway Musical LET IT BE

Words and Music by JOHN LENNON
and PAUL McCARTNEY

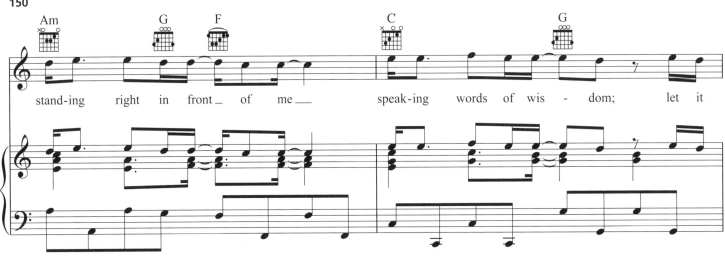

stand-ing right in front of me speak-ing words of wis - dom; let it

be. _____ let it be, _____ let it be, _____ let it be, _____

Instrumental ends

_____ let it be. _____ Whis-per words of wis - dom; let it be. _____

And when _____ the bro - ken-heart - ed peo - ple

And when _____ the night _____ is cloud - y, there is

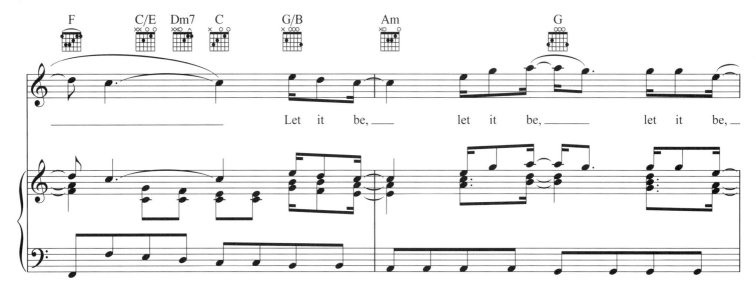

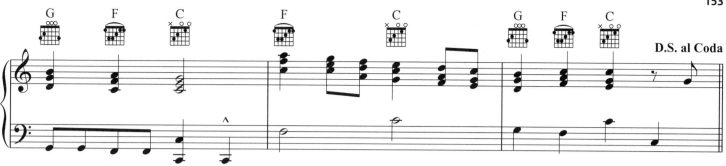

D.S. al Coda

CODA

Let it be, _____ let it be, _____ let it be, __

_____ let it be. _____ Whis-per words __ of wis - dom; let it be. __

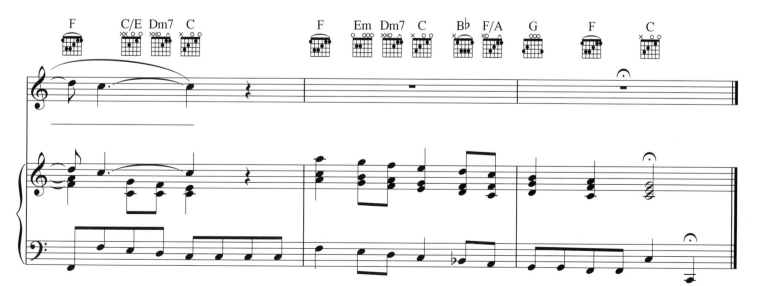

I WILL SURVIVE

featured in PRISCILLA, QUEEN OF THE DESERT

Words and Music by DINO FEKARIS
and FREDERICK J. PERREN

I BELIEVE
from the Broadway Musical THE BOOK OF MORMON

Words and Music by TREY PARKER,
ROBERT LOPEZ and MATT STONE
Vocal Arrangement by STEPHEN OREMUS

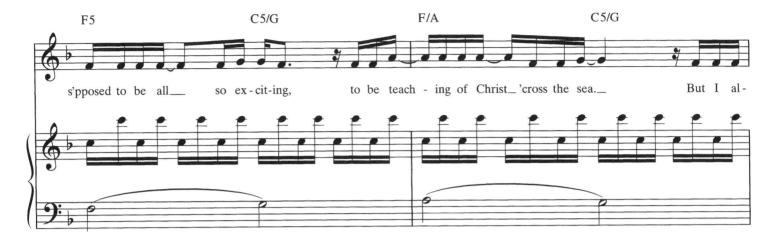

s'pposed to be all___ so ex-cit-ing, to be teach - ing of Christ___ 'cross the sea.___ But I al-

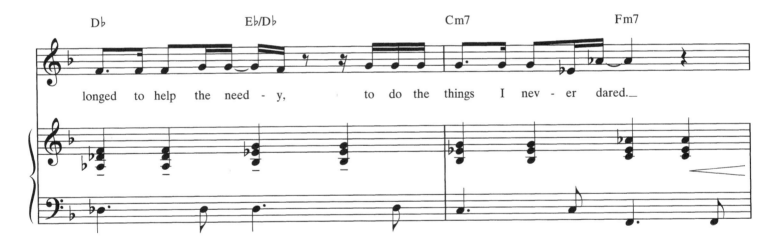

lowed my faith to be shak - en. Oh, what's the mat-ter with me? I've al-ways

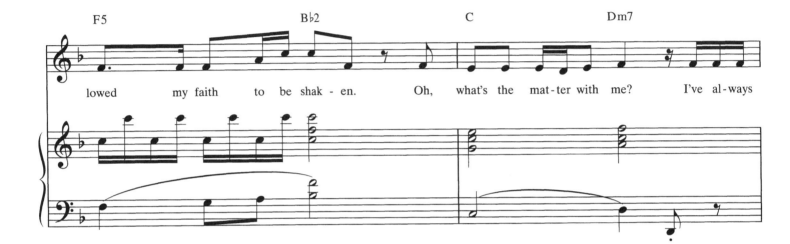

longed to help the need - y, to do the things I nev - er dared.___

This was the time for me to step up, so then why was I so scared? A

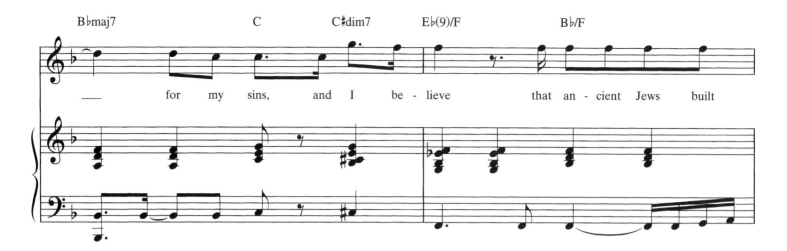

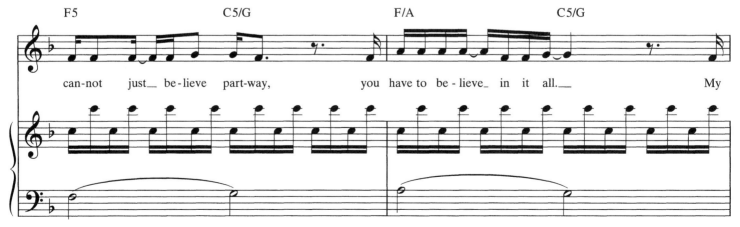

162

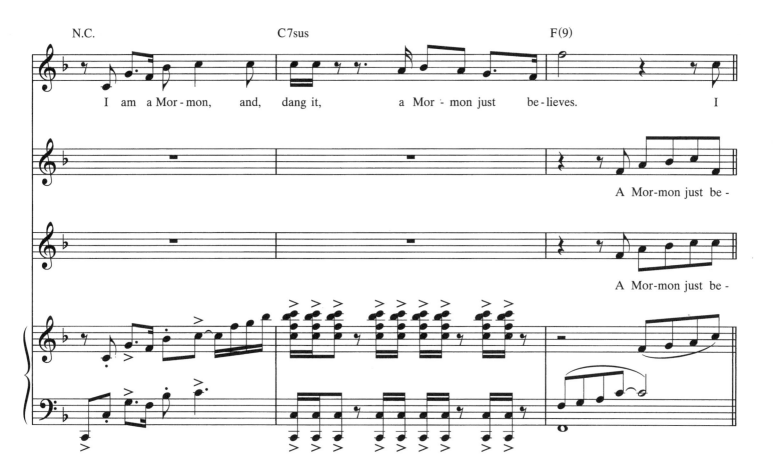

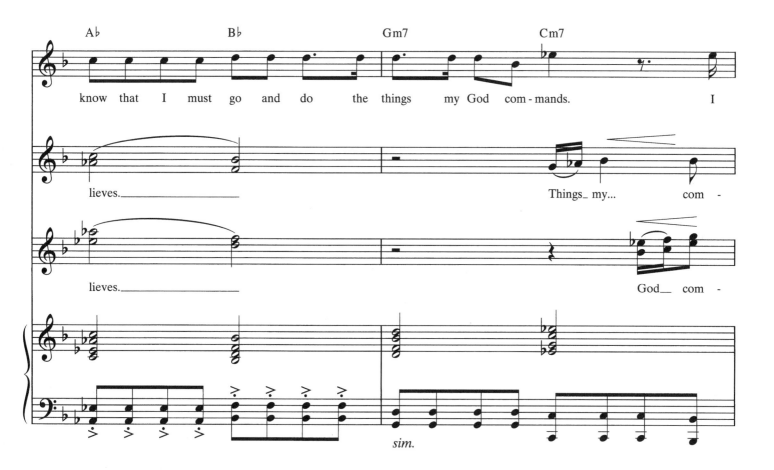

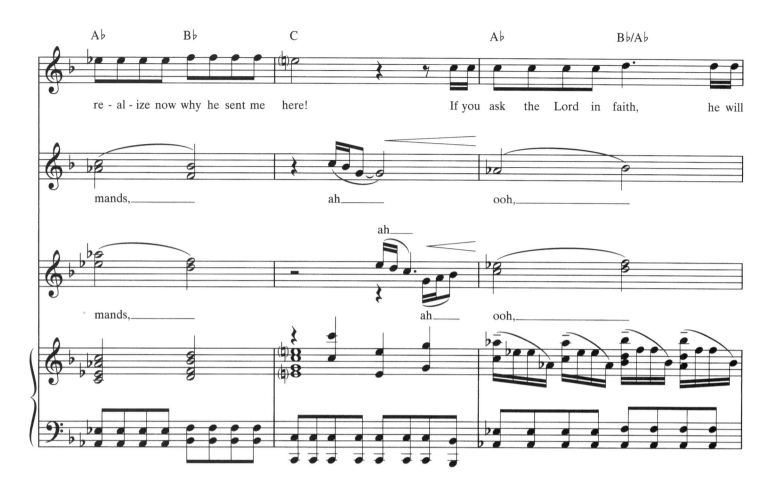

General: *The fuck is this?*

IF THE WORLD SHOULD END

from SPIDER-MAN: TURN OFF THE DARK

Music and Lyrics by
BONO and THE EDGE

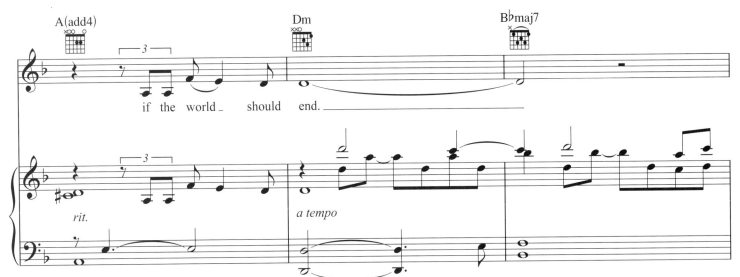

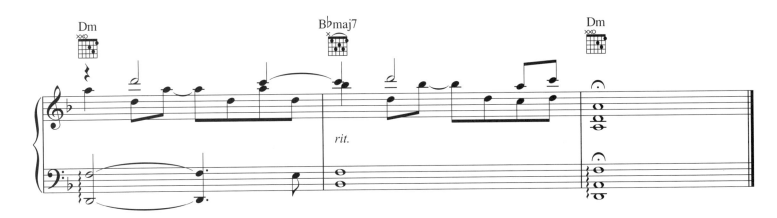

FALLING SLOWLY

from the Broadway Musical ONCE

Words and Music by GLEN HANSARD
and MARKETA IRGLOVA

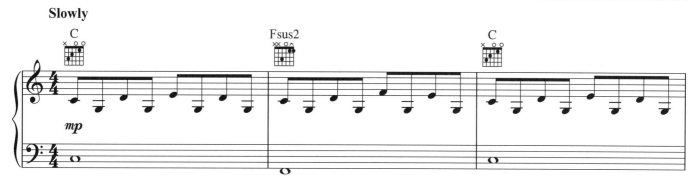

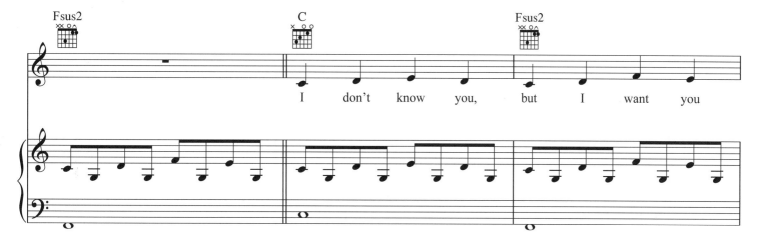

I don't know you, but I want you all the more for that. Words fall through me and

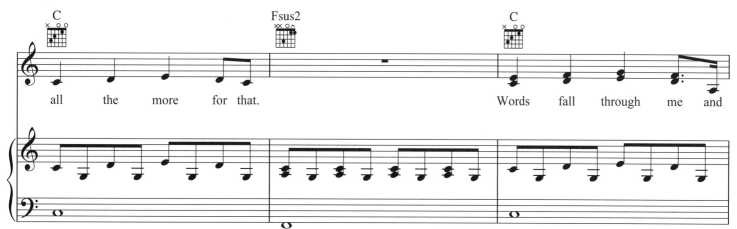

al - ways fool me, and I can't re - act.

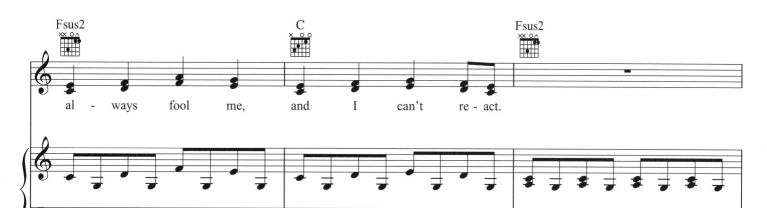

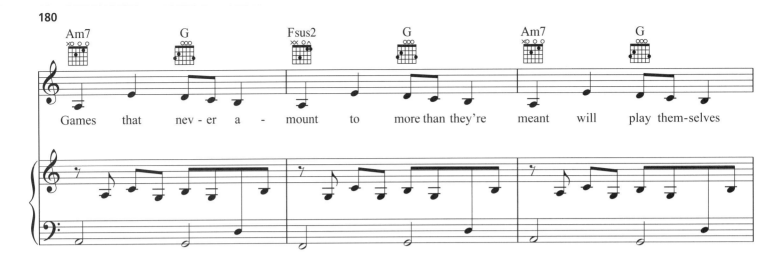

Games that nev-er a - mount to more than they're meant will play them-selves

out. ___ Take this sink - ing

boat and point it home; we've still got time. _____

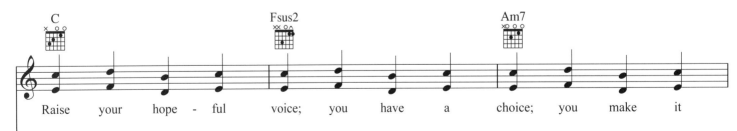

Raise your hope - ful voice; you have a choice; you make it

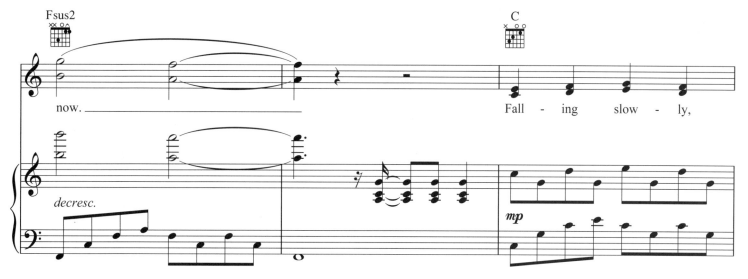

Fsus2   C

now. _____ Fall - ing slow - ly,

decresc.   *mp*

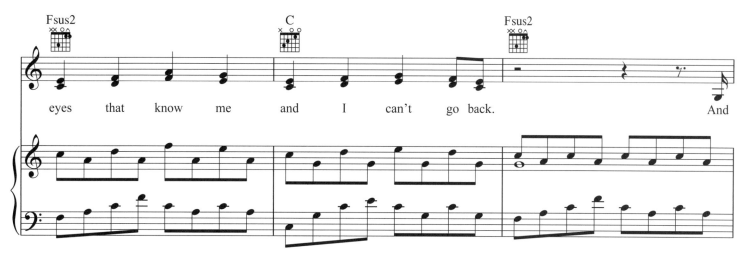

Fsus2   C   Fsus2

eyes that know me and I can't go back. And

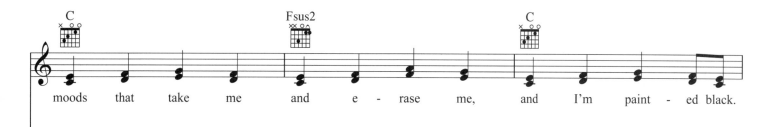

C   Fsus2   C

moods that take me and e - rase me, and I'm paint - ed black.

Fsus2   Am   Em/G   Fsus2   G

Well, you have suf-fered e - nough and warred with your -

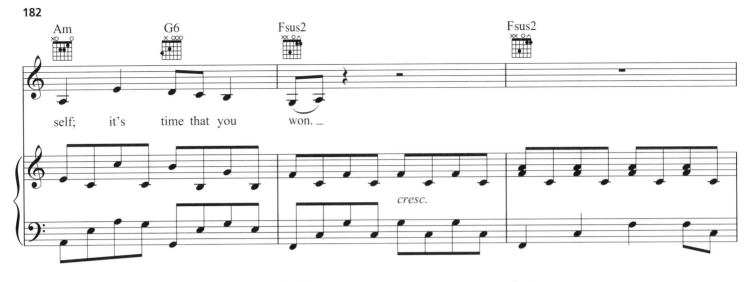

self;   it's   time that you   won. _

Take   this   sink - in'   boat   and   point   it   home,   we've   still   got

cresc.

time. _____   Raise   your   hope - ful   voice;   you   have   a

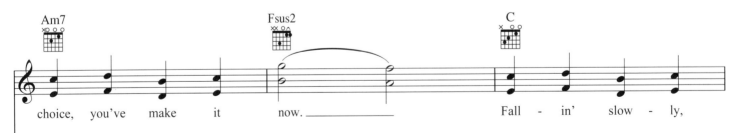

choice,   you've   make   it   now. _____   Fall - in'   slow - ly,

Now you're gone. ___

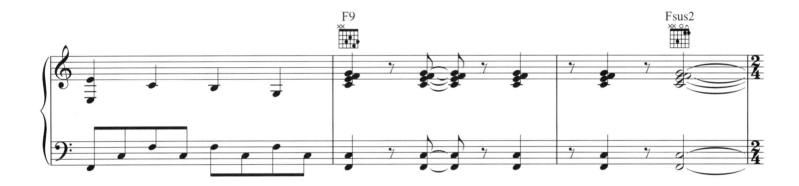

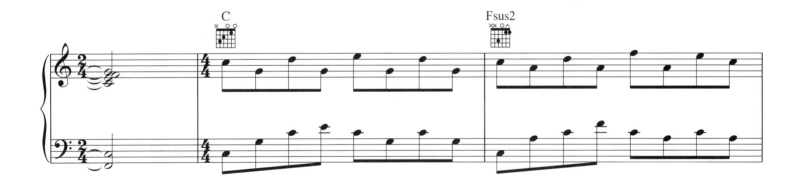

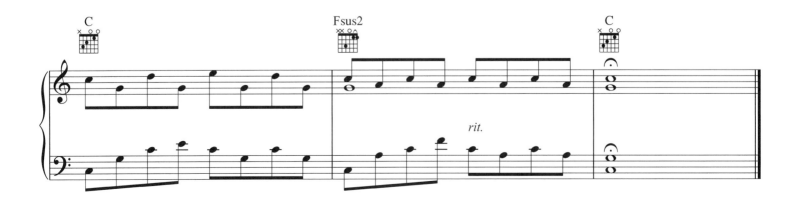

rit.

SANTA FE

from Walt Disney's NEWSIES - THE MUSICAL

Music by ALAN MENKEN
Lyrics by JACK FELDMAN

Driving (in 2)

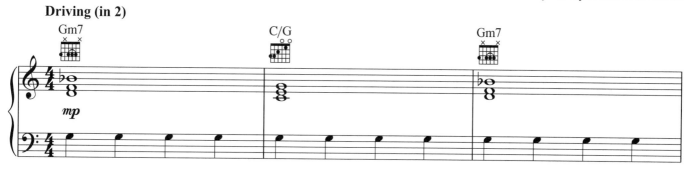

JACK:
Folks, we fi - n'lly got a head - line: "New - sies

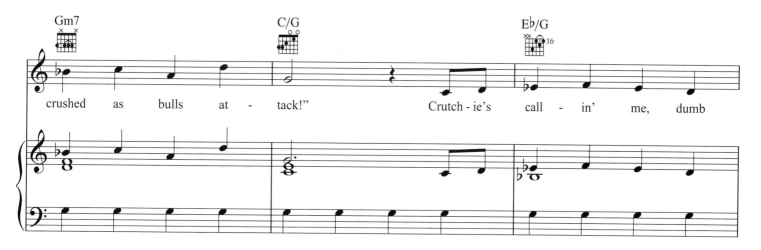

crushed as bulls at - tack!" Crutch - ie's call - in' me, dumb

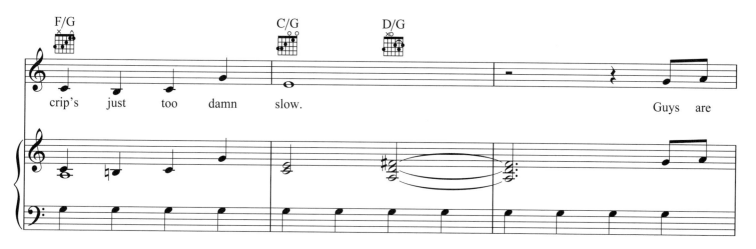

crip's just too damn slow. Guys are

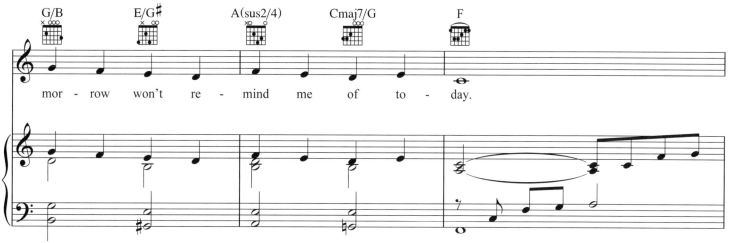

mor - row won't re - mind me of to - day.

When the cit - y's fi - n'lly sleep - in', and the

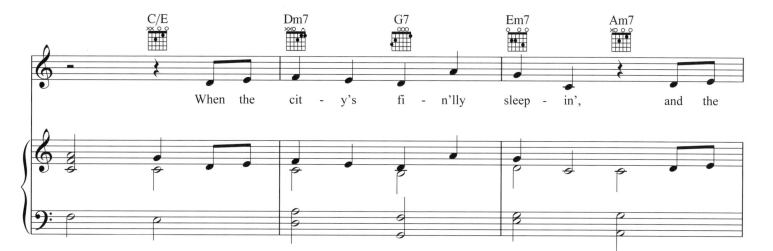

moon looks old and gray, I get on the train that's

dim.

mp dolce

bound for San - ta Fe. And I'm

cresc.

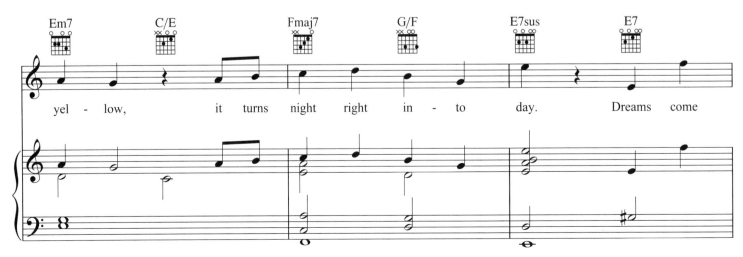

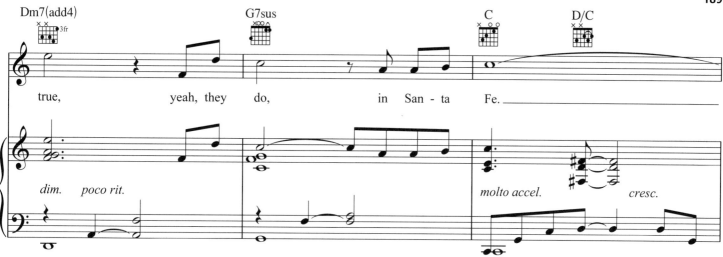

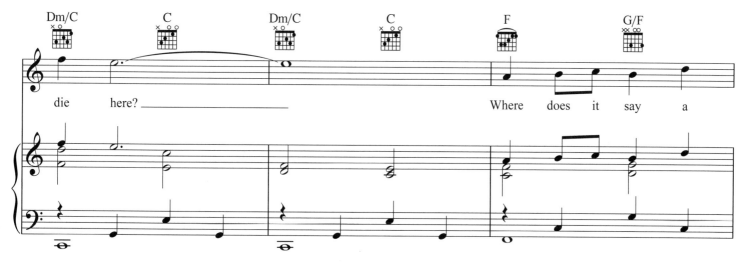

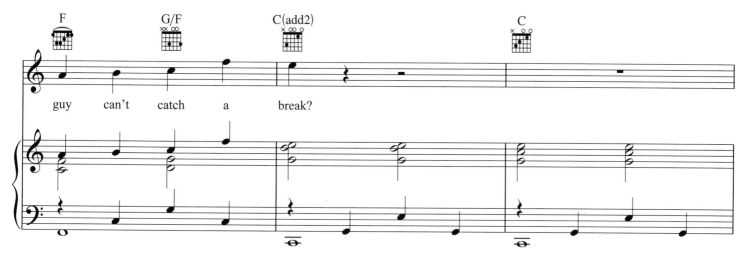

Why should you on-ly take what you're giv-en? Why should you spend your

whole life liv-in' trapped where there ain't no fu - ture,

e - ven at sev - en - teen, break - in' your back for

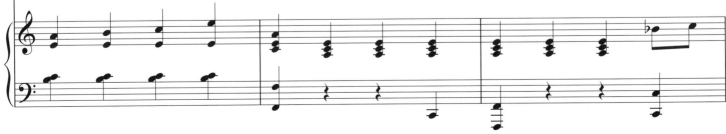

some - one el - se's sake? If the

Solidly, slightly faster

poco accel.

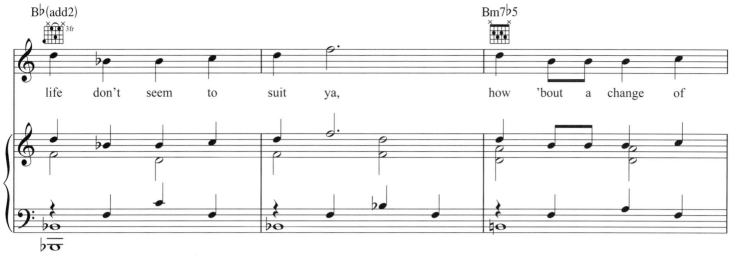

life don't seem to suit ya, how 'bout a change of

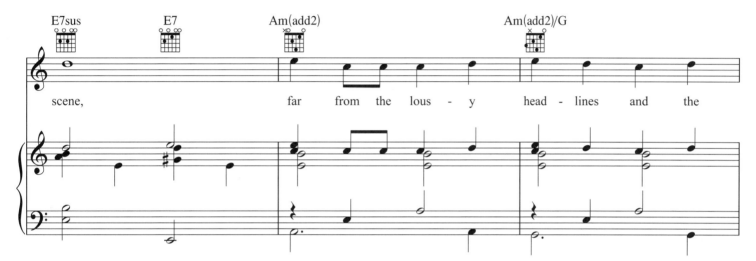

scene, far from the lous - y head - lines and the

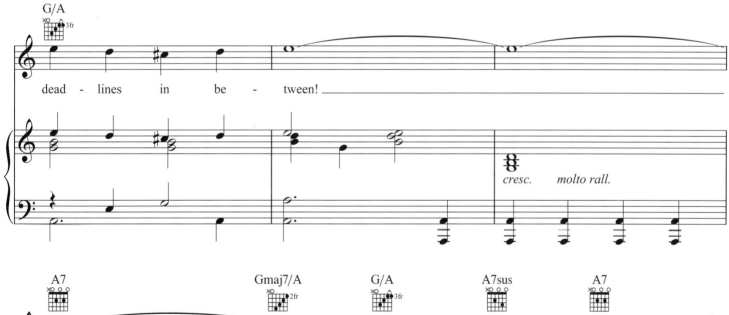

dead - lines in be - tween! _____

cresc. *molto rall.*

_____ San - ta

cresc.

Broadly, in 4

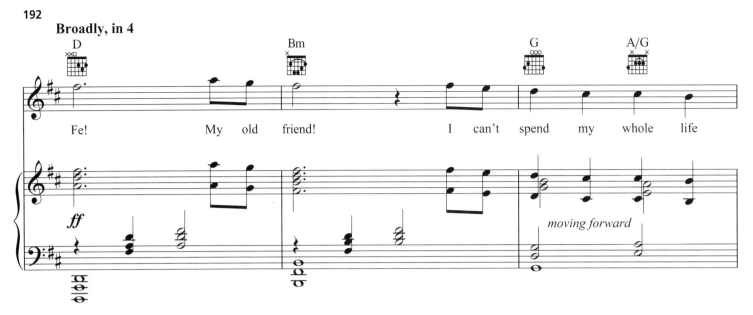

Fe! My old friend! I can't spend my whole life

ff

moving forward

dream-in', though I know that's all I seem in-clined to

do. I ain't get-tin' an-y

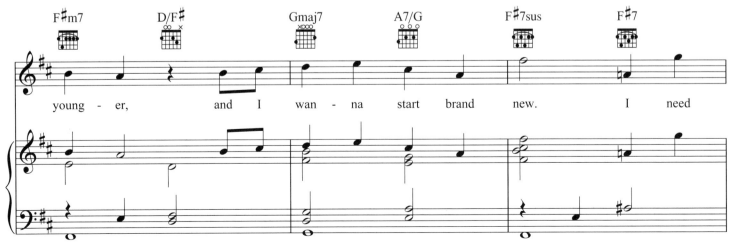

young-er, and I wan-na start brand new. I need

More broadly

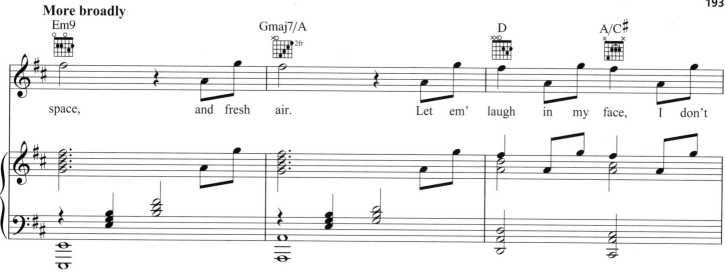

space, and fresh air. Let em' laugh in my face, I don't

care. Save my place, I'll be there…

rit. *dim.*

A tempo (poco rubato)

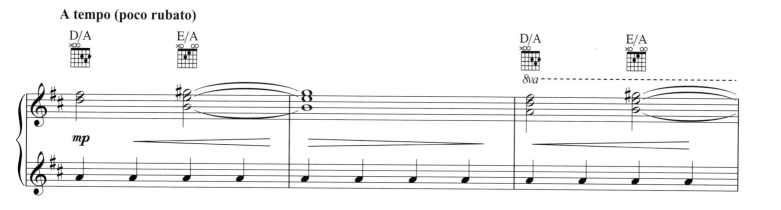

Just be real is all I'm ask - in', not some

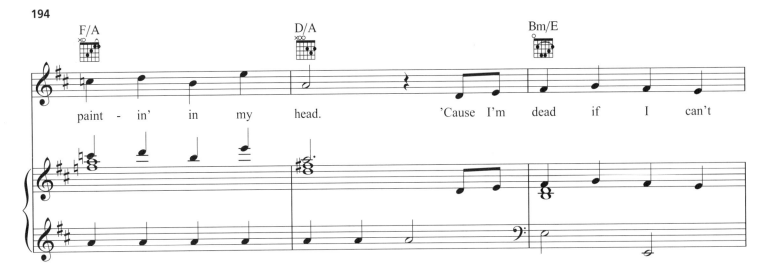

paint - in' in my head. 'Cause I'm dead if I can't

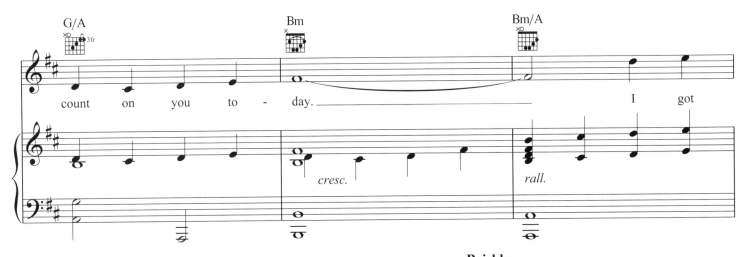

count on you to - day. _____ I got

noth - in', if I don't got San - ta Fe. _____

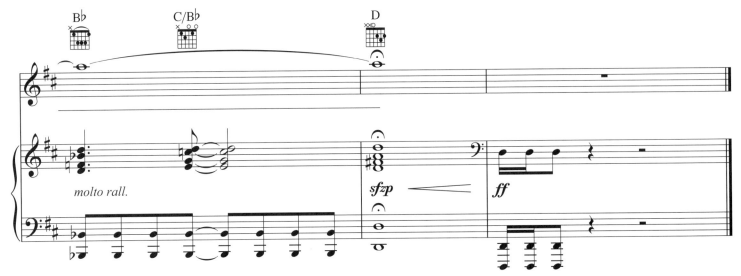

SOMEONE TO WATCH OVER ME

from OH, KAY!

Music and Lyrics by GEORGE GERSHWIN
and IRA GERSHWIN

There's a say-ing old Says that love is blind, Still we're of-ten told, "Seek and ye shall find." So I'm going to seek A cer-tain lad I've had in mind. Look-ing ev-'ry-where, Have-n't

found him yet; He's the big af-fair I can-not for-get.

On - ly man I ev - er Think of with re - gret.

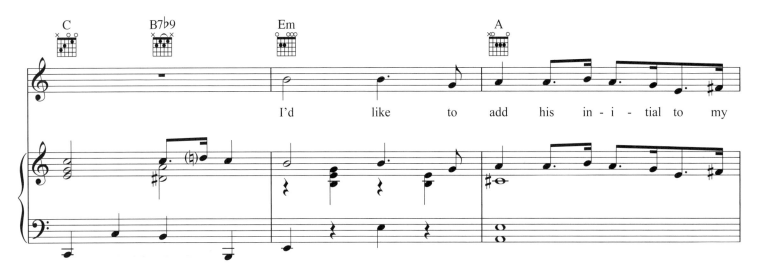

I'd like to add his in-i-tial to my

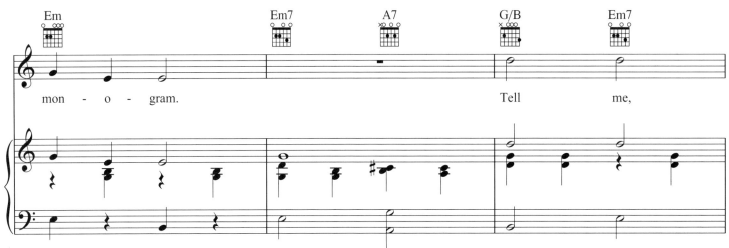

mon - o - gram. Tell me,

where is the shep-herd for this lost lamb?

There's a some-bod-y I'm long-ing to see. I hope that he

Turns out to be Some-one who'll watch o - ver

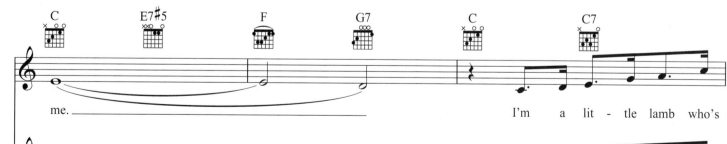

me. I'm a lit-tle lamb who's

lost in the wood. I know I could Al - ways be good

To one who'll watch o - ver me. _____

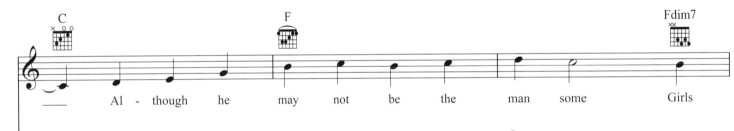

Al - though he may not be the man some Girls

think of as hand - some, To my heart he

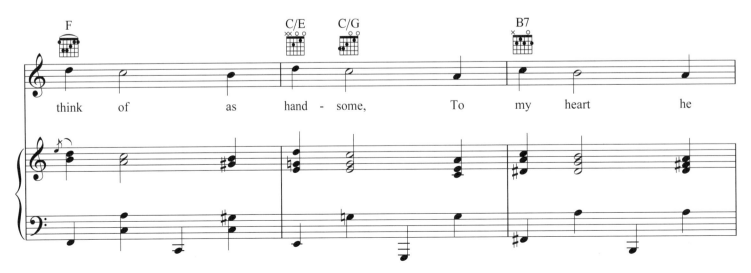

WHAT A MOTHER DOES
from A CHRISTMAS STORY - THE MUSICAL

Words and Music by BENJ PASEK
and JUSTIN PAUL

Moderately, in 1

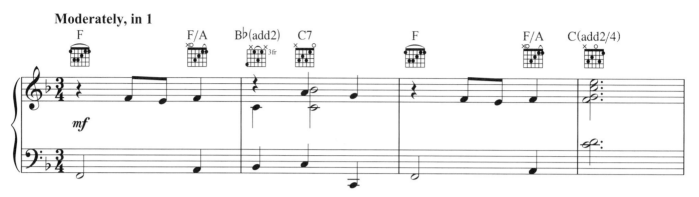

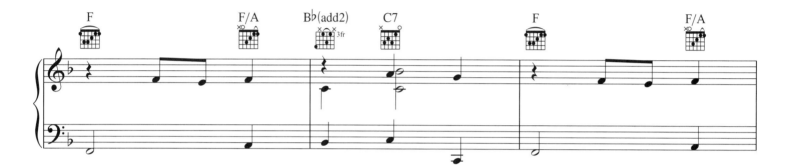

New stains on the rug,

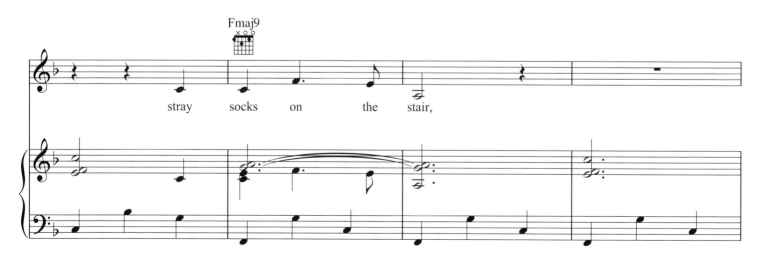

stray socks on the stair,

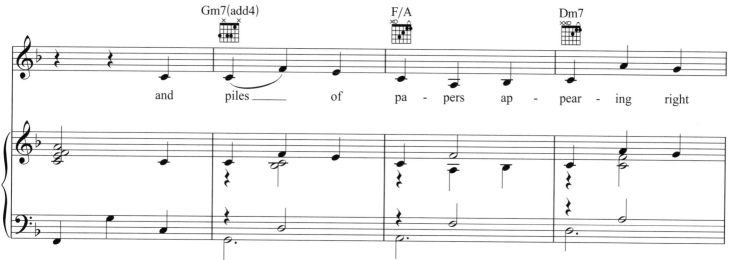

and piles _____ of pa - pers ap - pear - ing right

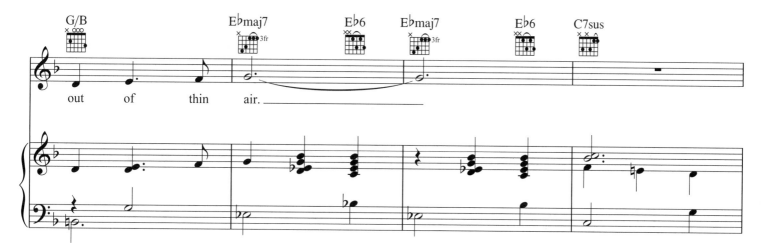

out of thin air. _____

But, the sheets have been washed,

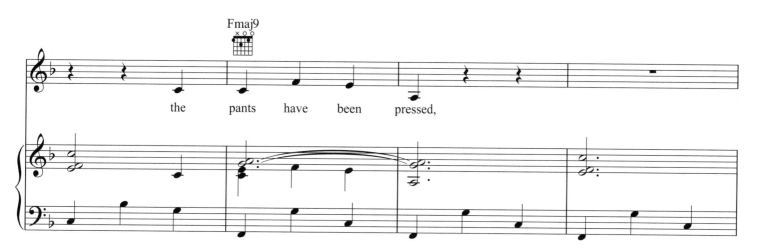

the pants have been pressed,

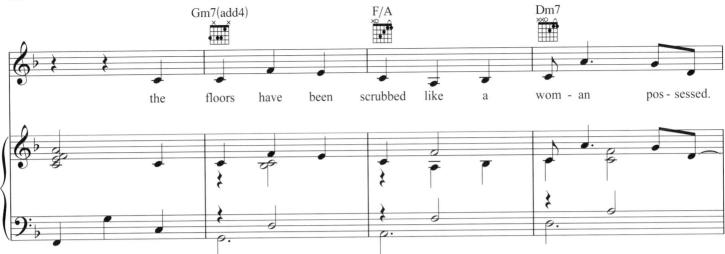

the floors have been scrubbed like a wom-an pos-sessed.

And we're stea-dy, and sta-ble, a meal on the

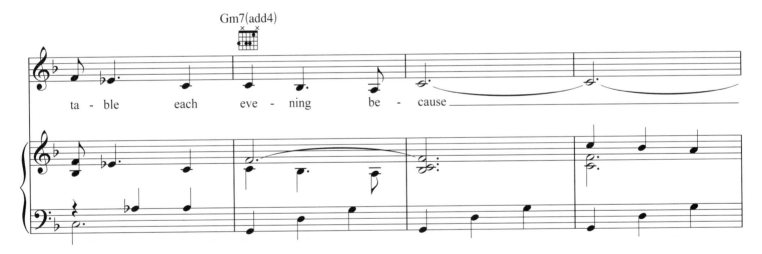

ta-ble each eve-ning be - cause _____

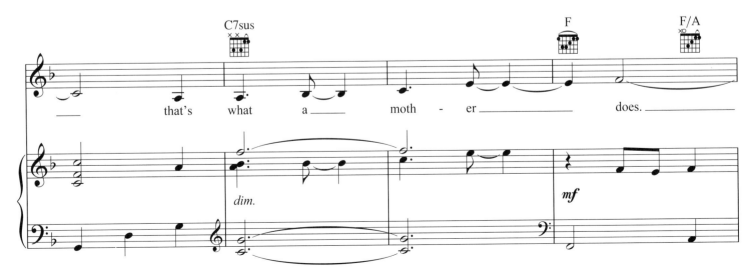

_____ that's what a _____ moth - er _____ does. _____

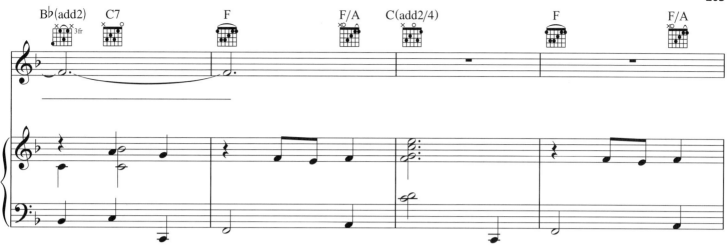

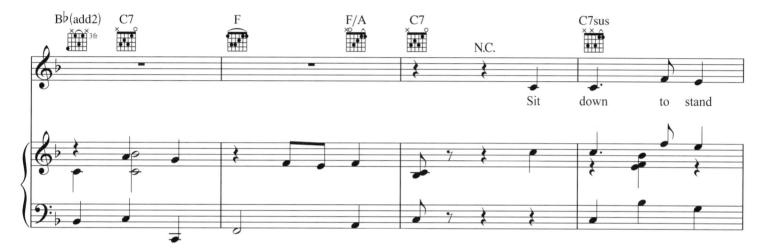

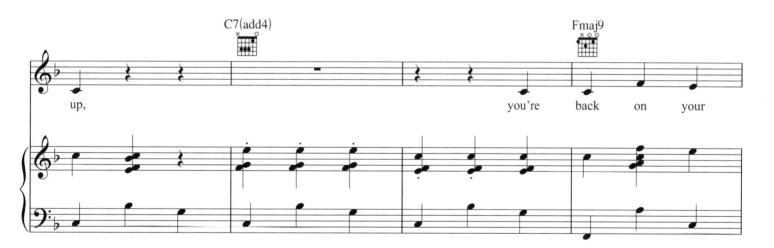

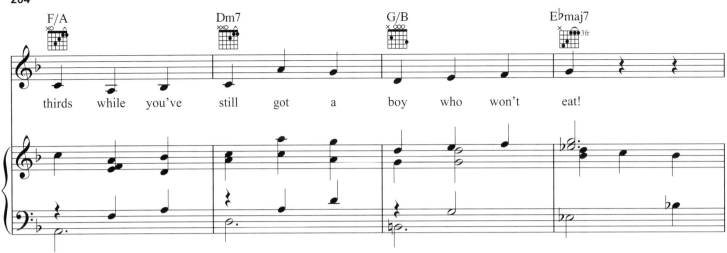

thirds while you've still got a boy who won't eat!

But, a mom has her ways,

a mom knows her kid.

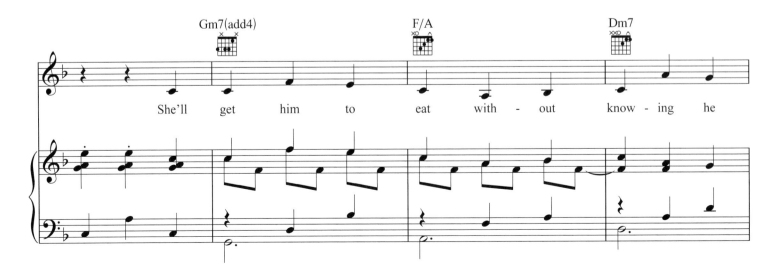

She'll get him to eat with - out know - ing he

did. It's just one of her tal - ents. She keeps life in

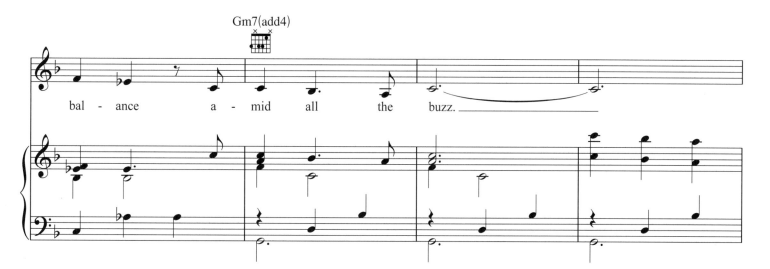

bal - ance a - mid all the buzz.

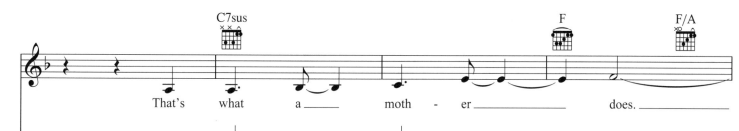

That's what a moth - er does.

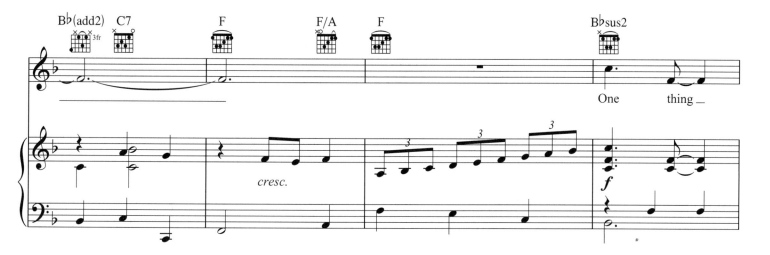

One thing

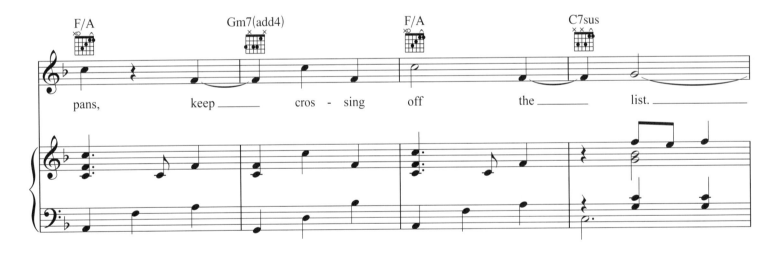

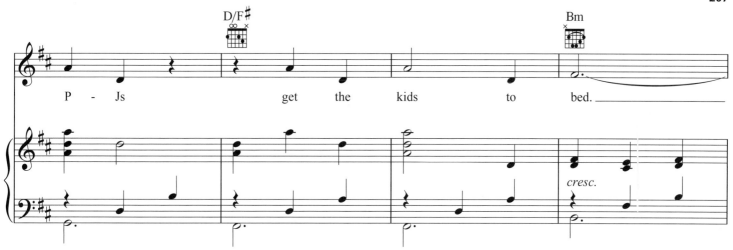

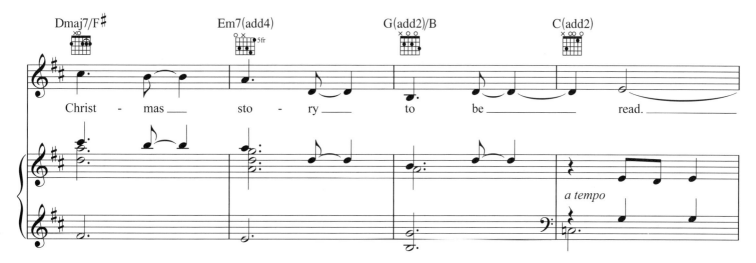

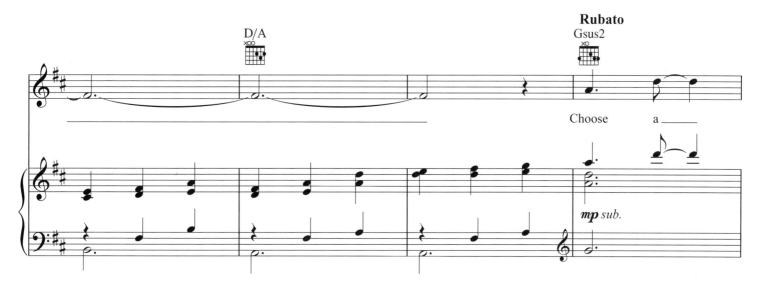

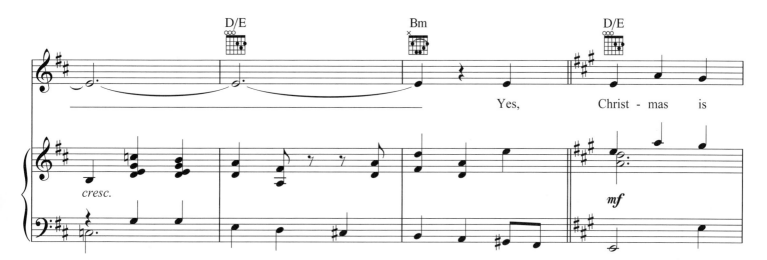

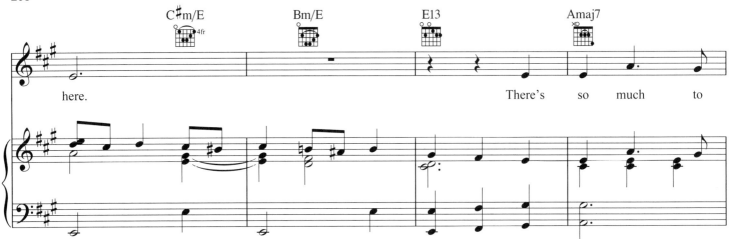

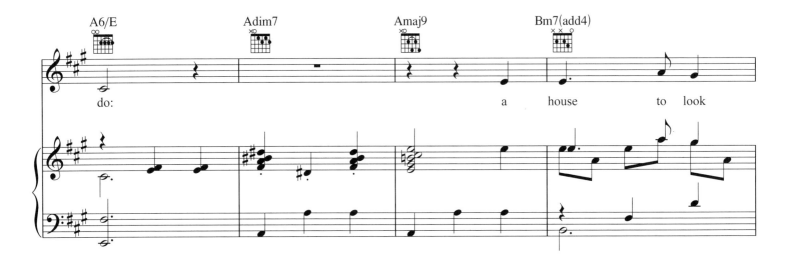

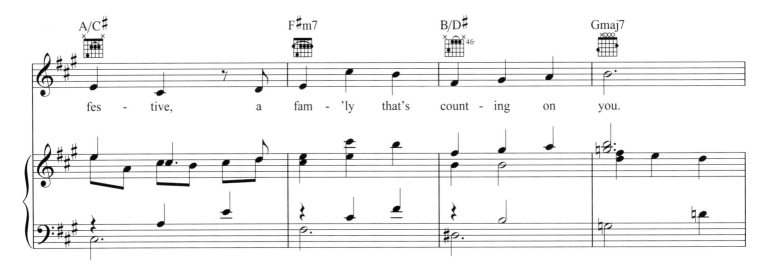

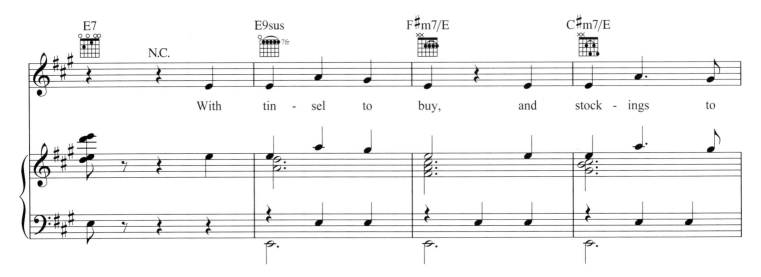

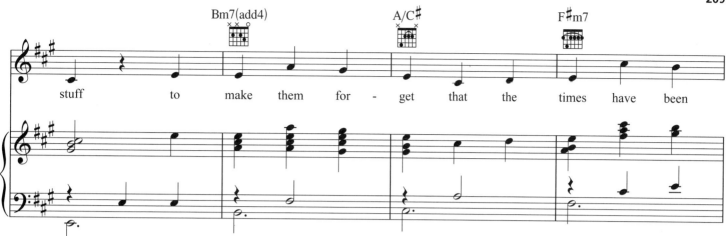

stuff to make them for - get that the times have been

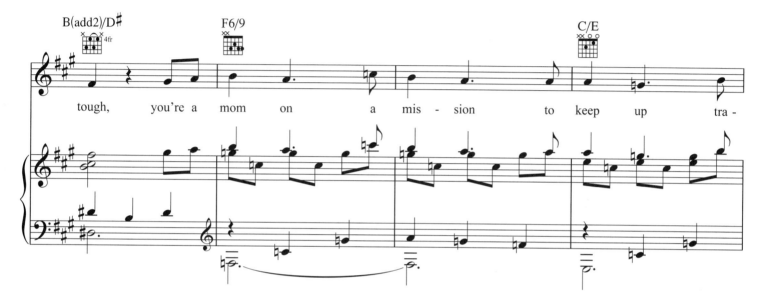

tough, you're a mom on a mis - sion to keep up tra -

di - tion. Cook - ies and car - ols and laugh - ter in

bar - rels, till you hear them say _____

you've made Christ - mas Day

F#m7   A(add2)/C#   Dmaj7

the ver - y best ___ Christ - mas ___ that

cresc.

Bm7(add4)   B/D#

there ev - er was. ___

8va

With resolve
Bm11

'Cause,   that's what a moth - er, ___

f

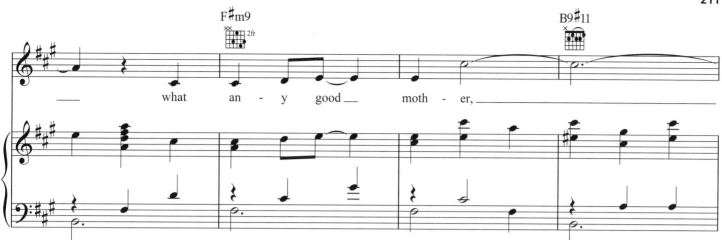

what an-y good moth-er,

that's what a moth

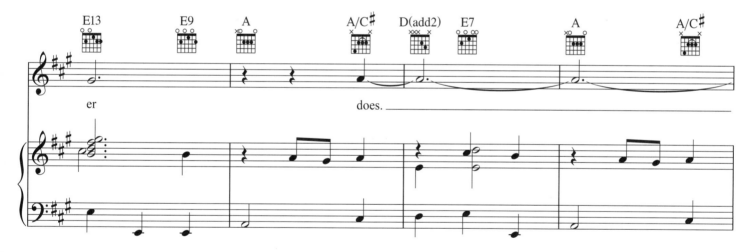

er does.

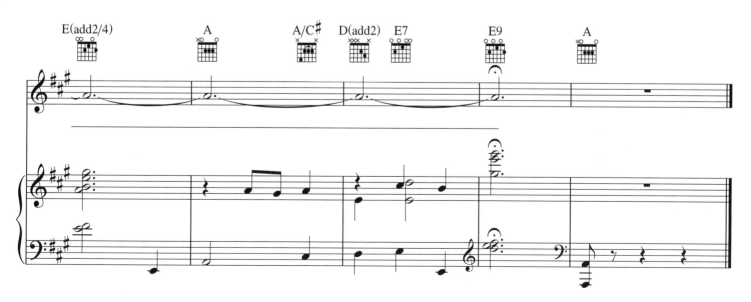

TEN MINUTES AGO
from CINDERELLA

Lyrics by OSCAR HAMMERSTEIN II
Music by RICHARD RODGERS

Tempo di Valse

Ten

min - utes a - go, I saw you, ____ I looked up when you

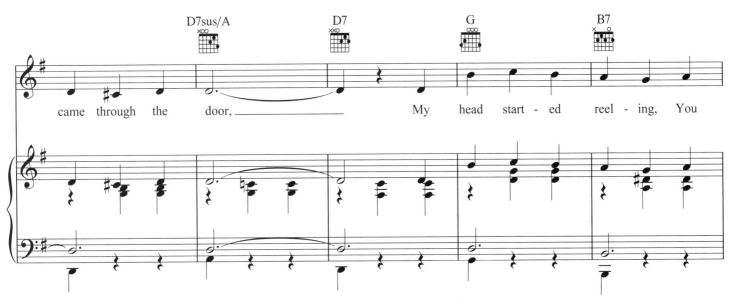

came through the door, ____ My head start - ed reel - ing, You

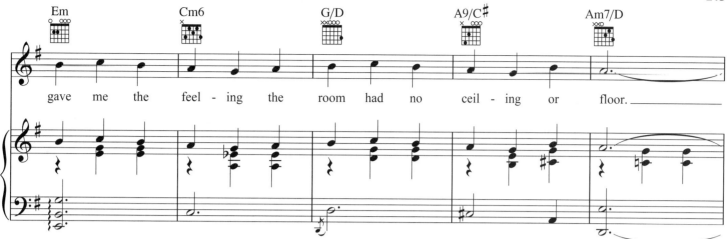

gave me the feel - ing the room had no ceil - ing or floor.

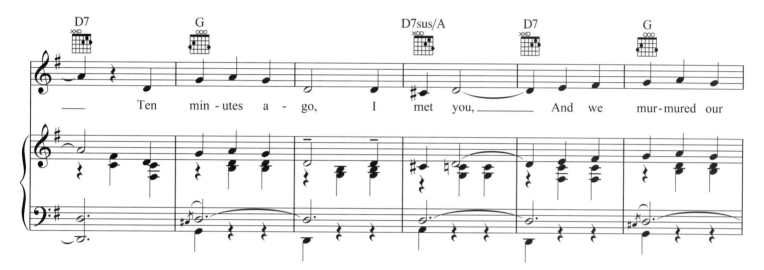

—— Ten min - utes a - go, I met you, ——— And we mur-mured our

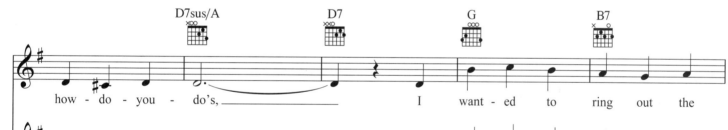

how - do - you - do's, ——————— I want - ed to ring out the

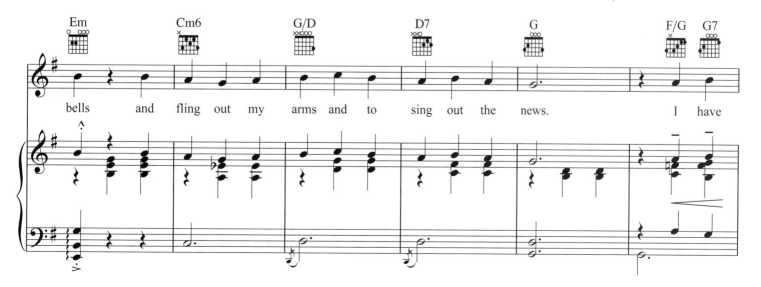

bells and fling out my arms and to sing out the news. I have

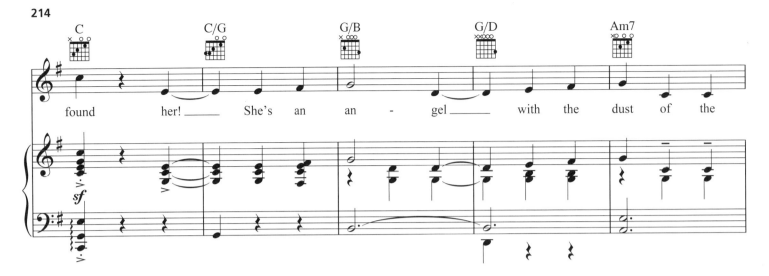

found her! _____ She's an an - gel _____ with the dust of the

stars in her eyes. We are danc - ing, we are fly - ing _____

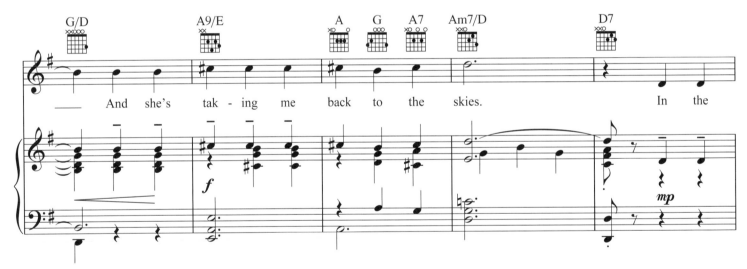

_____ And she's tak - ing me back to the skies. In the

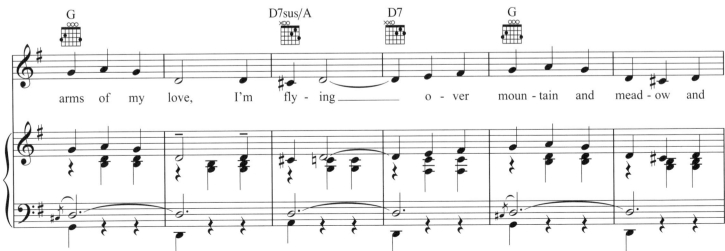

arms of my love, I'm fly - ing _____ o - ver moun - tain and mead - ow and

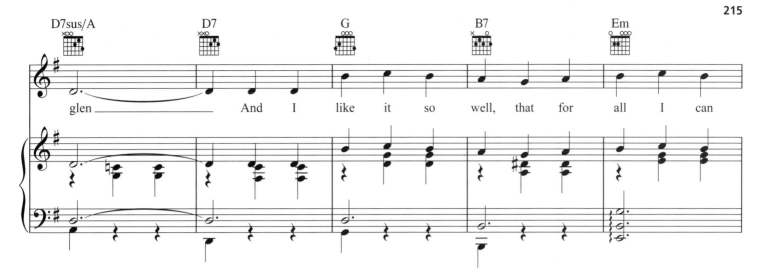

glen _____ And I like it so well, that for all I can

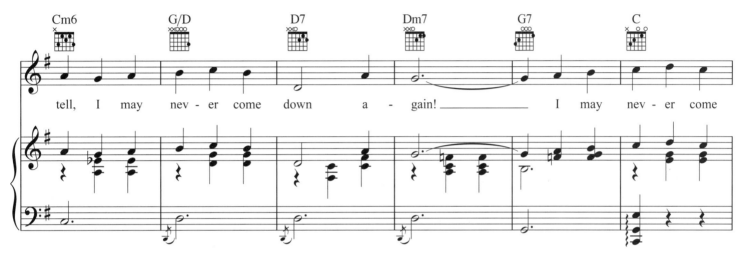

tell, I may nev-er come down a - gain! _____ I may nev-er come

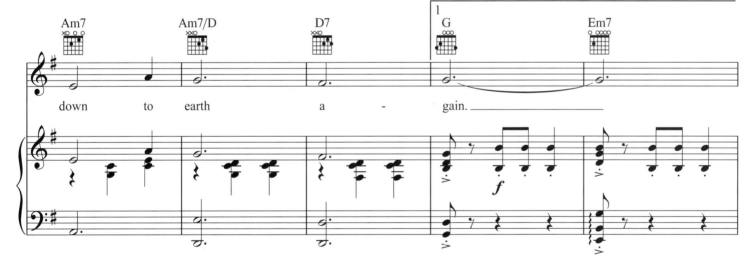

down to earth a - gain. _____

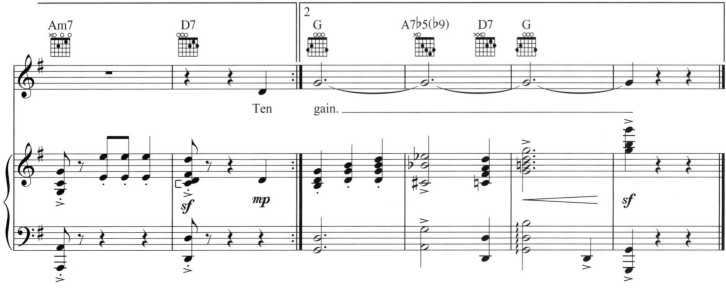

Ten gain. _____

Ain't No Mountain High Enough

from MOTOWN THE MUSICAL

Words and Music by NICKOLAS ASHFORD
and VALERIE SIMPSON

I DON'T NEED A ROOF

from BIG FISH

Music and Lyrics by
ANDREW LIPPA

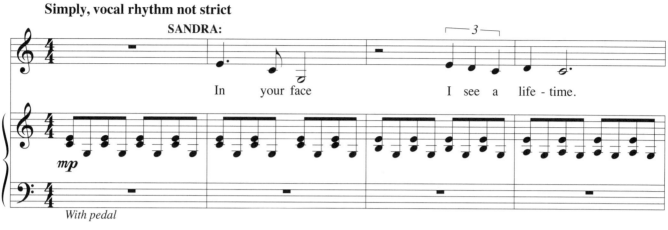

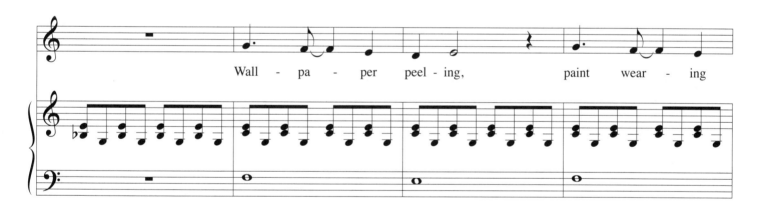

I don't need a roof to say I'm cov-ered.

I don't need a roof to know I'm home.

There could be a sin-gle shin-gle dan-gling o - ver-head.

I don't need a roof to make my

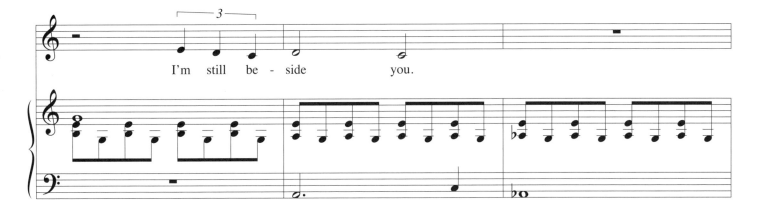

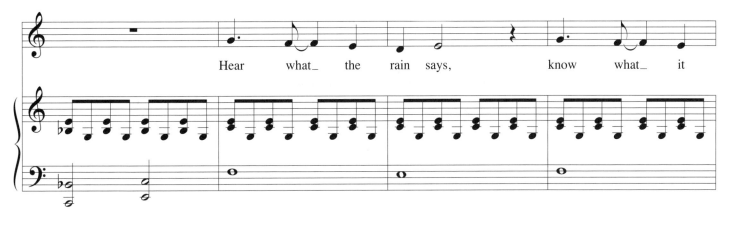

224

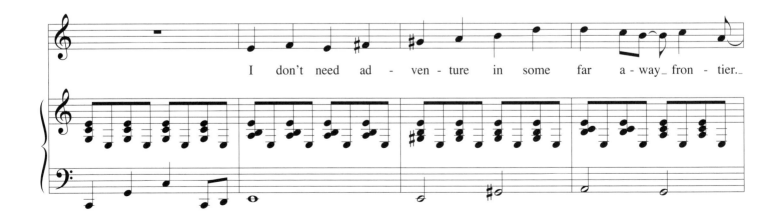

I don't need_ a roof__ to feel_ you

near. All I need_ is you,__ and you_ for - ev - er.

All I feel_ is true__ and ab - so - lute.

I don't need a le - gal deed to help me__ play my

part.   I   don't need___   a   roof___   to   hold___ my

heart.   Stay_____   with

me.   Stay_____   with

me._____

POISON IN MY POCKET

from A GENTLEMAN'S GUIDE TO LOVE AND MURDER

Music by STEVEN LUTVAK
Lyrics by ROBERT L. FREEDMAN and
STEVEN LUTVAK

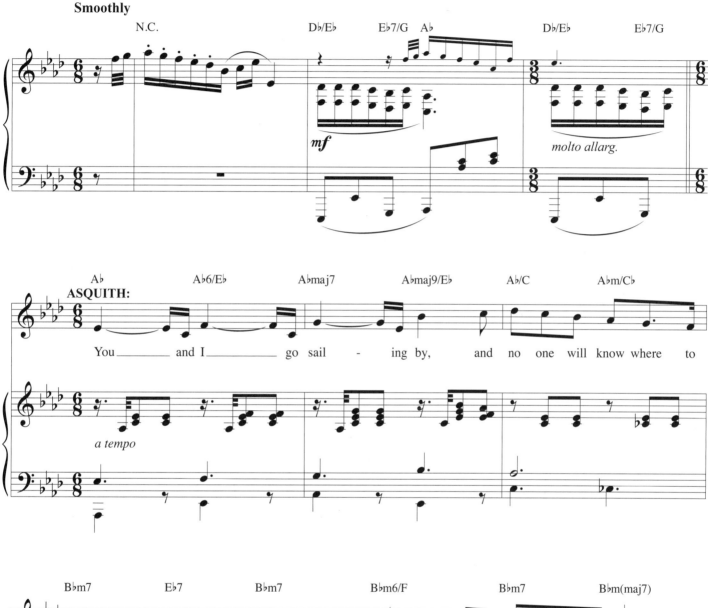

MONTY:

I am stand-ing here with poi-son in my pock-et, stand-ing on this fro-zen lit-tle dock, it seems that

I've just let them skate my op - por - tu - ni - ty a - way.

If I'd had the poise to put the poi-son in a pot of tea, or else a shot of gin, I would be

back a - mid the noise of Lon - don by the end of day. But,

I am stand-ing here with poi-son in my pock-et, one eye on the tar-get, one eye on the clock, it

bet-ter hap-pen soon be-fore I lose my nerve and run.

If I had a knife, I could have grabbed him, then dis-creet-ly knocked him on the head and stabbed him, not to

men-tion what I would have done if I had had a gun. Then a-gain, the

237

238

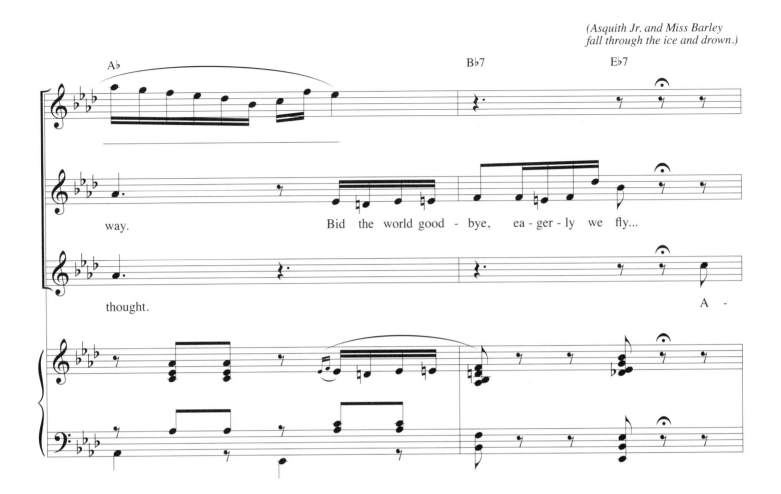

(Asquith Jr. and Miss Barley
fall through the ice and drown.)

way.

Bid the world good - bye, ea - ger - ly we fly...

thought.

A -

way!⎯⎯⎯

All of this is, frank - ly, eas - i - er than I had thought!

HAL LEONARD:
Your Source for the Best of Broadway

THE BEST EVER
COLLECTION
ARRANGED FOR PIANO, VOICE AND GUITAR

150 of the Most Beautiful Songs Ever
150 ballads
00360735 ....$27.00

150 More of the Most Beautiful Songs Ever
150 songs
00311318 ....$29.99

More of the Best Acoustic Rock Songs Ever
69 tunes
00311738 ....$19.95

Best Acoustic Rock Songs Ever
65 acoustic hits
00310984 ....$19.95

Best Big Band Songs Ever
68 big band hits
00359129 ....$17.99

Best Blues Songs Ever
73 blues tunes
00312874 ....$19.99

Best Broadway Songs Ever
83 songs
00309155 ....$24.99

More of the Best Broadway Songs Ever
82 songs
00311501 ....$22.95

Best Children's Songs Ever
96 songs
00310358 ....$19.99

Best Christmas Songs Ever
69 holiday favorites
00359130 ....$24.99

Best Classic Rock Songs Ever
64 hits
00310800 ....$22.99

Best Classical Music Ever
86 classical favorites
00310674 (Piano Solo) $19.95

The Best Country Rock Songs Ever
52 hits
00118881 ....$19.99

Best Country Songs Ever
78 classic country hits
00359135 ....$19.99

Best Disco Songs Ever
50 songs
00312565 ....$19.99

Best Dixieland Songs Ever
90 songs
00312326 ....$19.99

Best Early Rock 'n' Roll Songs Ever
74 songs
00310816 ....$19.95

Best Easy Listening Songs Ever
75 mellow favorites
00359193 ....$19.95

Best Gospel Songs Ever
80 gospel songs
00310503 ....$19.99

Best Hymns Ever
118 hymns
00310774 ....$18.99

Best Jazz Standards Ever
77 jazz hits
00311641 ....$19.95

More of the Best Jazz Standards Ever
74 beloved jazz hits
00311023 ....$19.95

Best Latin Songs Ever
67 songs
00310355 ....$19.99

Best Love Songs Ever
65 favorite love songs
00359198 ....$19.95

Best Movie Songs Ever
71 songs
00310063 ....$19.99

Best Praise & Worship Songs Ever
80 all-time favorites
00311057 ....$22.99

More of the Best Praise & Worship Songs Ever
76 songs
00311800 ....$24.99

Best R&B Songs Ever
66 songs
00310184 ....$19.99

Best Rock Songs Ever
63 songs
00490424 ....$18.99

Best Songs Ever
72 must-own classics
00359224 ....$24.99

Best Soul Songs Ever
70 hits
00311427 ....$19.99

Best Standards Ever, Vol. 1 (A-L)
72 beautiful ballads
00359231 ....$17.99

Best Standards Ever, Vol. 2 (M-Z)
73 songs
00359232 ....$17.99

More of the Best Standards Ever, Vol. 1 (A-L)
76 all-time favorites
00310813 ....$17.99

More of the Best Standards Ever, Vol. 2 (M-Z)
75 stunning standards
00310814 ....$17.95

Best Torch Songs Ever
70 sad and sultry favorites
00311027 ....$19.95

Best Wedding Songs Ever
70 songs
00311096 ....$19.95

HAL•LEONARD
CORPORATION
7777 W. BLUEMOUND RD. P.O. BOX 13819 MILWAUKEE, WI 53213

Visit us online for complete songlists at
www.halleonard.com